Contents

Meeting Individual Needs: Advanced Students

Houghton Mifflin Reading's materials for reaching all learners are a time-saving system of instruction. With this group of handbooks you can turn your attention to specific needs in your classroom—to advanced students, students who are struggling below level, or students who are learning English—while other students work independently. The Challenge, Extra Support, and English Language Learners handbooks are each tied to the core instruction in *Houghton Mifflin Reading*. For independent work, the *Classroom Management Handbook* provides meaningful activities related to literature selections and to core skills.

As a group, the handbooks for reaching all learners:

- help you manage your classroom and organize your time effectively
- provide excellent, additional instruction
- give you the resources you need to help all students achieve grade level expectations

Challenge Handbook Overview

The *Challenge Handbook* has been developed to help you deliver instructional activities to advanced learners that will extend their experiences with the literature and skills in *Houghton Mifflin Reading*, challenging them to use higher-level thinking in interactive and meaningful ways.

The activities are presented in a five-day plan that uses the Challenge Masters and teacher support in this handbook and that also recommends use of the provisions for Challenge students in other components of *Houghton Mifflin Reading*. Your Teacher's Edition provides Challenge suggestions at point of use and in the Theme Resources section.

Students should be challenged to engage in higher-level thinking and explorations that are integrated with the learning of the larger group.

Students Who Need a Challenge

Students for whom the Challenge Activities are intended are those who are often called gifted and talented or advanced learners. They meet one or more of these criteria:

- They have mastered the core content and are ready for a challenge; they may be English Language Learners if they have adequate proficiency English.

- They are reading and writing one or two grades above their designated grade.

- They have a record of task-commitment and independence and can work at a more advanced level.

See the *Teacher's Assessment Handbook* for recommendations for identifying students who are ready for a challenge. Group students flexibly, as the *Classroom Management Handbook* recommends, to provide a challenge to as many students as can profit by it and to encourage ideas to flow among mixed-ability groups.

Preparing Students to Work Independently

Prepare students to work independently—individually, in pairs, or in small groups. Work with students to develop guidelines for independent work. Plan with them some strategies to use if they are stuck and need help. Make sure they know where to find material resources. (See also the *Classroom Management Handbook*.)

Challenge students benefit from the interaction of working in small groups or pairs as well as from working individually. The inquiry portion of a project often involves interviewing and interaction with others. Sharing their results with the larger groups of classmates also keeps Challenge students involved with others.

Emphasize the need for students to stay committed to the task and to plan their time. If some part of the project requires using resources outside the classroom, discuss how that work can be accommodated. Some activities, both full-week projects and shorter ones, may engage a student's interest and warrant more time. Allow extensions that are profitable, but insist that students set goals and plan for an end date.

In planning with students, be realistic about opportunities for presenting their results. A Challenge Master activity may include a range of suggestions for sharing, but you may decide to limit the audience, the time, and the place.

Some students respond well to challenges mainly because of their ability to stay committed to a task.

Instruction for Challenge Students

Advanced learners need instruction or coaching to channel their talents and to focus their ideas. Often, for new tasks, they need specific information beyond the regular classroom instruction for their grade. They need guidance to extend what they can already do and to complete products of high quality. The activities in this handbook provide that, in directions and Tips for students and in the recommendations for brief coaching and instruction on the pages for you.

Plan time each week to give the preparation provided, particularly for the major project, and check in with students occasionally to provide additional coaching.

Effective Ways to Challenge Students

Accelerate students' learning and ask them to explore concepts and content in greater depth. Ask of students a higher level of thinking, encourage flexible and creative thinking, and promote problem solving. You will do this by using Activities in the Challenge Handbook, which

- are integrated with the content of the literature and skills in the themes so that students can relate to material they have already encountered, explore it more deeply, and think flexibly and more broadly about it

- are interdisciplinary, often developing a relationship between theme content and other curriculum areas

- are inquiry-based in helping students learn how to learn, to do research and to summarize, synthesize, or otherwise use what they have learned in the inquiry phase of their project

- encourage wider reading, including books, articles, and Internet resources, and ask students to collect data and ideas in various ways, such as interviewing within their classroom and beyond

- engage students in the processes at the highest levels of Bloom's Taxonomy—application, analysis, synthesis, and evaluation

- ask students to recognize and solve different types of problems

- provide exercises in multiple perspectives, such as asking students to write a different version of a selection

- focus on a genre, asking students to compare selections or to write in the genre of a selection

- provide opportunities for students to challenge each other, through games, discussions, or problem-solving situations

- call upon students to apply learning strategies, to set goals, and to plan their projects

- enable students to make choices within projects

Many advanced learners, while talented, need coaching to stay focused.

Features of the Challenge Handbook

The Walkthrough on pages vi–ix gives a visual overview. Each major selection has these features:

- A major project that students work on for the week is on the first page of both the student's and the teacher's material. Students begin by planning and brainstorming; they move on to information-gathering, drafting, or creating—doing the project; and finally they present and share it. The teacher's page suggests how to pace the activity over five days. It provides recommendations for coaching or instruction to give students, usually on the first day, and often on the third day, and ends with suggestions for helping students present and share their projects. There are suggestions for your involvement on Days 1, 3, and 5.

- There are two shorter activities on the second page, each of which can be completed in about one hour. These cover the same range of content, skills, and modes as the week-long projects, but they are less ambitious in terms of the scope and time required.

- Connecting/Comparing Literature is a suggestion to the teacher to have students compare works of the same genre and apply comprehension skills.

- Additional Activities is a list of resources available for *Houghton Mifflin Reading*. It provides a reminder of those activities that are planned as Challenges throughout the Teacher's Editions as well as listing other books and media in the program. These resources are summarized in the Assignment Planner in the *Classroom Management Handbook*. You can select those you wish to assign to Challenge students while you are working with other groups.

Blackline Masters

At the back of this handbook are

- the student Blackline Masters for the Challenge Activities, for you to duplicate for each student.

- Graphic Organizer Masters that are called for in Challenge Activities; they can be used for other activities. They include story maps, conclusions charts, problem-solution charts, and other graphics that can help students organize their thinking.

See the Walkthrough on the following pages for more information.

The Challenge activities provide structure to encourage growth: goals and tips for students, and expected outcomes to help you direct and evaluate their work.

Walkthrough

To the Teacher

This walkthrough will familiarize you with the five-day plan that is provided for Challenge students for each selection in this level of *Houghton Mifflin Reading.* Annotations in this walkthrough introduce the major parts of the activities for five days.

Day-by-Day Plan for the Major Project

On Day 1 students plan their project; they brainstorm, do research, or gather information and ideas. On Days 2–4, they continue to gather ideas, they carry out their plan, and they share the results.

Instruction or Coaching for Challenges

Instruction or coaching is provided to enable students to work effectively at a challenging level and to ensure high-quality work.

Expected Outcome

The Expected Outcome shows the quality and quantity of work expected from a Challenge student.

Sharing

Sharing, publishing, or presenting the result is the culmination of every five-day Challenge project.

Content Area; Materials

- Any content-area connection is noted.
- Materials needed, other than paper and pencil, are listed. Some activities need Graphic Organizer Masters, which are in the Blackline Masters section at the back of this handbook.

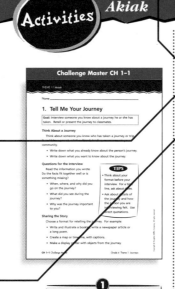

SELECTION 1: *Akiak*

Activities

Challenge Master CH 1–1

1. Tell Me Your Journey 150 MINUTES INDIVIDUAL
(Social Studies)
Materials: encyclopedia, atlas, drawing paper, crayons, and markers

DAY 1

Think About a Journey
Have students research the route of the journey so that they can ask questions that refer to the locations visited. Have students:

- List places/sites that the traveler is likely to have visited.
- Prepare questions that invite the traveler to describe reactions to those places. For example: *What were your thoughts when you saw the Grand Canyon?*

English Language Learners: Review the use of an encyclopedia as a reference source. Discuss with students how to use the information in an entry.

DAY 2

Students continue to work on this project.

DAY 3

Questions for the Interview
Check with students on their progress.

- Remind students that their presentation should accurately reflect the facts and the interviewee's thoughts.
- Tell students to do further research or questioning to fill in any gaps.

DAY 4

Students continue to work on this project.

DAY 5

Sharing the Story
Tell students to choose a format that clearly presents what they have. Students can combine two formats if they desire.

Expected Outcome

A good interview will include

✔ two or three important things that happened during the journey and the traveler's reactions

✔ important details

 THEME 1: **Journeys**

Time; Grouping

- Approximate amount of time an activity takes
- Recommendations for grouping.

2. A New Point of View

60 MINUTES INDIVIDUAL PAIR

- Have students first choose the new point of view and then find a scene that works for retelling.
- Have students think about how they will present the scene. Point out that details may change because of their character's different point of view.

English Language Learners: Explain that to write from a character's point of view means to imagine what that character would see and feel.

3. Follow That Story! *60 MINUTES* INDIVIDUAL

Materials: daily newspapers or on-line news sources and dictionary

- Students should refer to their news stories for accuracy.
- Have students review the news stories and use a dictionary or other reference source to make sure they understand all the words.

Additional Independent Work

Connecting/Comparing Literature

Have students compare the Leveled Reader selection *The Trail Home* with the anthology selection *Akiak*, using what they have learned about Story Structure. Students may discuss or write about their comparisons.

Other Activities

- Theme 1 Assignment Cards 1, 2, 3
- TE p. 50, Literature Discussion
- TE p. 57, Social Studies
- TE p.57E, Challenge Word Practice

- TE pp. R9, R17, Challenge
- Education Place: www.eduplace.com More activities related to *Akiak*
- Accelerated Reader®, *Akiak*

---

② Expected Outcome

A good retelling will
- ✔ include details only from the new point of view
- ✔ reflect the character's feelings about the events

③ Expected Outcome

A good paper will include
- ✔ a clear comparison of two different news articles
- ✔ a description of how each writer uses quotations
- ✔ an explanation of which story the student liked the most

Challenge Master CH 1-2

THEME 1/ *Akiak*

Name

2. A New Point of View

Goal: Retell a story scene from a new point of view.

Change the narration in *Akiak.* Choose a scene from the story and write it from the point of view of one of the other characters. For example:
- Mick or another musher
- Akiak or another dog
- the man who let Akiak out the back door

TIPS
- Think about details that bring a story to life. What would the character see, hear, and remember?
- Think about the character's feelings in that scene. How would those feelings affect the way he or she tells the story?

3. Follow That Story!

Goal: Read two news stories and compare them in writing.

Find two news stories on the same topic. Write a short paper that compares how reporters describe the events and how they use quotations in each. Tell which news story you like best and explain why.

TIPS
- Look for facts about the topic used in both stories to help you make comparisons.
- Make a list of people quoted in each story and what they said.
- Jot down details that support your choice for best story.

Grade 4 Theme 1: Journeys   *Challenge Master CH 1-2*

SELECTION 1: *Akiak* 3

The Activities on Masters

The three numbered activities on these pages appear on two blackline masters to be used during the week. The first master has the major project for the week. The two shorter activities on the second Challenge Master can be done any time during the week.

English Language Learners

Adaptations are provided when activities need to be made more accessible to English Language Learners.

Connecting/Comparing Literature

Connecting/ Comparing Literature is a standard recommendation to have students compare works of literature, applying the comprehension skill they learn with this selection.

Other Activities

Other Activities are challenging independent work that can be found elsewhere in materials for *Houghton Mifflin Reading*, referenced here as a reminder to use them.

Facsimile of Challenge Master

Heading identifies the student's blackline master. A reduced facsimile is provided here. Full-size Challenge Masters are in the Blackline Masters section of this handbook.

Challenge Masters

Full-size blackline masters are in the Blackline Masters section of this handbook.

Goal

The Goal describes a student's task. Point out the Goal, and preview the students' Activity page with them.

Tips

Tips help students produce work of high quality.

Sharing

Students are usually able to choose their format for sharing.

Challenges

Questions or instructions lift activities to a challenging level.

THEME 1/*Akiak*

Name_____

1. Tell Me Your Journey

Goal: Interview someone you know about a journey he or she has taken. Retell or present the journey to classmates.

Think About a Journey

Think about someone you know who has taken a journey or trip. It could be a parent, relative, friend, teacher, or someone in your community.

- Write down what you already know about the person's journey.
- Write down what you want to know about the journey.

Questions for the Interview

Read the information you wrote. Do the facts fit together well or is something missing?

- When, where, and why did you go on the journey?
- What did you see during the journey?
- Why was the journey important to you?

TIPS

- Think about your format before your interview. For a time line, ask about dates.
- Ask about details of the journey and how the person you are interviewing felt. Use direct quotations.

Sharing the Story

Choose a format for retelling the journey. For example:

- Write and illustrate a booklet; write a newspaper article or a long poem.
- Create a map or time line, with captions.
- Make a display center with objects from the journey.

Grade 4 Theme 1: Journeys

Copyright © Houghton Mifflin Company. All rights reserved.

Activities 2 and 3

These two shorter activities can be done any time during the week.

THEME 1/*Akiak*

Name _____

2. A New Point of View

Goal: Retell a story scene from a new point of view.

Change the narration in *Akiak*. Choose a scene from the story and write it from the point of view of one of the other characters. For example:

- Mick or another musher
- Akiak or another dog
- the man who let Akiak out the back door

TIPS

- Think about details that bring a story to life. What would the character see, hear, and remember?

- Think about the character's feelings in that scene. How would those feelings affect the way he or she tells the story?

3. Follow That Story!

Goal: Read two news stories and compare them in writing.

Find two news stories on the same topic. Write a short paper that compares how reporters describe the events and how they use quotations in each. Tell which news story you like best and explain why.

TIPS

- Look for facts about the topic used in both stories to help you make comparisons.

- Make a list of people quoted in each story and what they said.

- Jot down details that support your choice for best story.

Copyright © Houghton Mifflin Company. All rights reserved.

Grade 4 Theme 1: Journeys

Challenge Master **CH 1-2**

Challenges

A skill applied is often more advanced than expected at this grade level.

Numbering of Masters

The numbering identifies the master as CH (Challenge Handbook) and gives the theme number followed by the number of the master in the sequence of Challenge Masters for this theme.

Theme 1

CHALLENGE ACTIVITIES FOR

Journeys

Selections

1 Akiak

2 Grandfather's Journey

3 Finding the Titanic

4 By the Shores of
Silver Lake

Activities

Challenge Master CH 1–1

THEME 1/*Akiak*

Name_____

1. Tell Me Your Journey

Goal: Interview someone you know about a journey he or she has taken. Retell or present the journey to classmates.

Think About a Journey

Think about someone you know who has taken a journey or trip. It could be a parent, relative, friend, teacher, or someone in your community.

- Write down what you already know about the person's journey.
- Write down what you want to know about the journey.

Questions for the Interview

Read the information you wrote. Do the facts fit together well or is something missing?

- When, where, and why did you go on the journey?
- What did you see during the journey?
- Why was the journey important to you?

Sharing the Story

Choose a format for retelling the journey. For example:

- Write and illustrate a booklet; write a newspaper article or a long poem.
- Create a map or time line, with captions.
- Make a display center with objects from the journey.

TIPS

- Think about your format before your interview. For a time line, ask about dates.
- Ask about details of the journey and how the person you are interviewing felt. Use direct quotations.

CH 1–1 Challenge Master   Grade 4 Theme 1: Journeys

---

① Expected Outcome

A good interview will include

✔ two or three important things that happened during the journey and the traveler's reactions

✔ important details

---

1. Tell Me Your Journey   150 MINUTES   INDIVIDUAL
(Social Studies)

Materials: encyclopedia, atlas, drawing paper, crayons, and markers

DAY 1

Think About a Journey

Have students research the route of the journey so that they can ask questions that refer to the locations visited. Have students:

- List places/sites that the traveler is likely to have visited.
- Prepare questions that invite the traveler to describe reactions to those places. For example: *What were your thoughts when you saw the Grand Canyon?*

English Language Learners: Review the use of an encyclopedia as a reference source. Discuss with students how to use the information in an entry.

DAY 2

Students continue to work on this project.

DAY 3

Questions for the Interview

Check with students on their progress.

- Remind students that their presentation should accurately reflect the facts and the interviewee's thoughts.
- Tell students to do further research or questioning to fill in any gaps.

DAY 4

Students continue to work on this project.

DAY 5

Sharing the Story

Tell students to choose a format that clearly presents what they have. Students can combine two formats if they desire.

2. A New Point of View

60 MINUTES   INDIVIDUAL   PAIR

- Have students first choose the new point of view and then find a scene that works for retelling.
- Have students think about how they will present the scene. Point out that details may change because of their character's different point of view.

English Language Learners: Explain that to write from a character's point of view means to imagine what that character would see and feel.

3. Follow That Story!   60 MINUTES   INDIVIDUAL

Materials: daily newspapers or on-line news sources and dictionary

- Students should refer to their news stories for accuracy.
- Have students review the news stories and use a dictionary or other reference source to make sure they understand all the words.

Additional Independent Work

Connecting/Comparing Literature

Have students compare the Leveled Reader selection *The Trail Home* with the anthology selection *Akiak,* using what they have learned about Story Structure. Students may discuss or write about their comparisons.

Other Activities

- Theme 1 Assignment Cards 1, 2, 3
- TE p. 50, Literature Discussion
- TE p. 57, Social Studies
- TE p.57E, Challenge Word Practice

- TE pp. R9, R17, Challenge
- Education Place: www.eduplace.com More activities related to *Akiak*
- Accelerated Reader®, *Akiak*

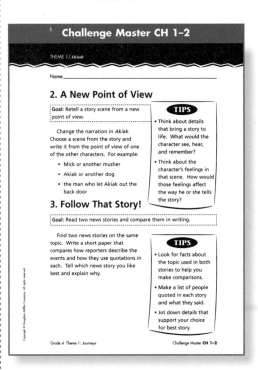

2

Expected Outcome

A good retelling will

✔ include details only from the new point of view

✔ reflect the character's feelings about the events

3

Expected Outcome

A good paper will include

✔ a clear comparison of two different news articles

✔ a description of how each writer uses quotations

✔ an explanation of which story the student liked the most

Activities

Challenge Master CH 1–3

THEME 1/*Grandfather's Journey*

Name_____

1. Story Circle

Goal: Learn a story from another country or culture and share it with the class.

Find a Common Theme

Find examples of stories from different cultures that share a theme or subject, such as bravery, overcoming problems, or wisdom.

- In a small group, discuss how the stories are alike and different.
- Each member of the group will then choose a story to share.
- Read and reread the story until you know it very well.
- List ways to present your story, such as reading it aloud, presenting it as a play, or using puppets.

Plan the Retelling

Meet with your story circle.

- Based on how much class time your story circle will have, decide how many minutes each member will have to share his or her story.
- Discuss the presentations the group is planning and decide on their order.

Share What You Know

Invite your classmates to hear your stories.

- Create a program naming the story presenters and their stories.
- Form a circle and tell your stories in order.

TIPS
- If your original story is long, choose an important part to read word for word. Summarize the rest.
- Rehearse your presentation in front of a mirror and/or with someone who can give you helpful comments.
- Have fun telling the story.

CH 1–3 Challenge Master   Grade 4 Theme 1: Journeys

① Expected Outcome

A good retelling will include

✔ a concise but complete presentation of a story

✔ an engaging, creative, and well-rehearsed retelling

✔ good storytelling techniques, such as speaking audibly, looking at the audience, and using gestures and body movements that enhance the story

1. Story Circle   150 MINUTES   INDIVIDUAL   SMALL GROUP
(Social Studies)

Materials: individual storybooks, anthologies, and miscellaneous materials for props (optional)

DAY 1

Find a Common Theme

Have students come to the group discussion after researching stories across cultures. Tell them to compare notes and then choose a story. Develop a shared theme by following these suggestions:

- Students should compare and discuss stories to avoid duplications. However, point out that stories often travel from country to country, so they may find similar plots and characters.
- Students should decide jointly on a theme and make sure each story contributes to it.

English Language Learners: Encourage students to share favorite stories from their own cultures. Have them include in their retelling words from their native languages and define them in context.

DAY 2

Students continue to work on this project.

DAY 3

Plan the Retelling

Check with students on the progress of their story preparation.

- Remind students that they must time their presentations so that everyone in the group can perform.
- Provide rehearsal time during the school day.

DAY 4

Students continue to work on this project.

DAY 5

Share What You Know

You may wish to invite family and community members or other classes to a story circle performance. Before doing so, have students evaluate their first performances so that they may improve their presentations.

2. Personal Poetry 60 MINUTES INDIVIDUAL

Materials: drawing paper, crayons, and markers

- Have students review the selection to find details and events that illustrate Grandfather's feelings.
- Remind students to change the point of view to first person singular: I, me, mine.

English Language Learners: You might want to pair students with English speakers.

3. *Over the Top of the World*

60 MINUTES INDIVIDUAL

(Challenge Theme Paperback)
Materials: reference materials

- Have students keep in mind that they are preparing this information for explorers who are experienced in other areas.
- Tell students that if they cannot find a definition for a term, they might draw a diagram to clarify the meaning.

Additional Independent Work

Connecting/Comparing Literature

Have students compare the Leveled Reader selection *Streets of Gold* with the anthology selection *Grandfather's Journey,* using what they have learned about Author's Viewpoint. Students may discuss or write about their comparisons.

Other Activities

- Challenge Theme Paperback, *Over the Top of the World*
- Theme 1 Assignment Cards 4, 5, 6
- TE p. 74, Literature Discussion
- TE p. 78, Word Study
- TE p. 79E, Challenge Word Practice

- TE pp. R6, R11, R19, Challenge
- Education Place: www.eduplace.com
  More activities related to *Grandfather's Journey*
- Accelerated Reader®, *Grandfather's Journey*

2

Expected Outcome

A good poem will include

✔ references to images, feelings, and events in the story itself

✔ word choices that express Grandfather's emotions

✔ a creative approach to language

3

Expected Outcome

A good list will include

✔ clear, understandable definitions

✔ explanations of why the information is important

✔ how the knowledge might be useful

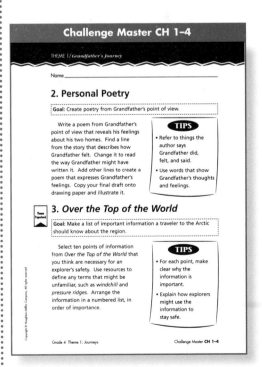

SELECTION 3:
Finding the Titanic

Challenge Master CH 1–5

THEME 1/*Finding the Titanic*

Name _____

1. Extra! Extra!

Goal: Recreate the front page of a local paper as it might have appeared on April 16, 1912, the day after the sinking of the *Titanic*.

Find the Facts

On April 16, 1912, newspapers around the world were full of the news of the sinking of the "unsinkable" *Titanic*.

- Find a current local or national newspaper to use as a model for your front page.
- Look for sources about the sinking, and make notes of the important details.
- Act as if you were the editor. Decide on a name for your newspaper, how many stories you would include, and how many photographs or illustrations would be on the front page.

Writing the Stories

Plan your front page. Each story should have an attention-grabbing headline and at least two supporting paragraphs. Then write one of the stories. Think about the focus of this story and how many details should be included.

TIPS

- Think about your audience; your story should keep your readers' attention.
- Write your story in short, informative sentences to deliver important information quickly.

Share What You Know

- Paste your story, illustrations, and photographs, on a large sheet of paper that will be your front page.
- Display your front page on the bulletin board along with other classmates' front pages.

CH 1–5 Challenge Master   Grade 4 Theme 1: Journeys

Copyright © Houghton Mifflin Company. All rights reserved.

① Expected Outcome

A good newspaper front page will include

- ✔ a story containing details about the event
- ✔ a clear presentation of facts
- ✔ intriguing story opener, headline, pictures, and captions

1. Extra! Extra!   150 MINUTES   INDIVIDUAL   PAIR
(Social Studies)

Materials: reference sources; newspaper samples; large, blank sheets of paper

DAY 1

Find the Facts

Show students different types/styles from the front pages of newspapers to give them a feel for what their front pages should look like. Tell students to use almanacs, encyclopedias, and history books as sources.

English Language Learners: You might want to brainstorm with students a list of possible story topics.

DAY 2

Students continue to work on this project.

DAY 3

Writing the Stories

Check with students on the progress of their story writing. Remind students they should think about answers to the questions *Who? What? Where? When? Why?* and *How?* before they write.

DAY 4

Students continue to work on this project.

DAY 5

Share What You Know

- Explain to students how to paste their stories in a two-column format.
- Photocopy each student's completed page to make a class set.

2. To Preserve or Not to Preserve?

60 MINUTES   INDIVIDUAL

- Have students review the selection to find details that might support their reasoning.
- Ask volunteers to read their essays. Then poll the rest of the class to see what they think. Discuss important points made.

3. Diorama 60 MINUTES   INDIVIDUAL

Materials: clean recycled materials and scraps that can be used to represent the wreckage; sand, or cat litter, for the ocean floor; cartons/boxes to hold the diorama

Tell students to cite any reference sources they use.

Additional Independent Work

Connecting/Comparing Literature

Have students compare the Leveled Reader selection *The Greatest Electrician in the World* with the anthology selection *Finding the* Titanic, using what they have learned about Text Organization. Students may discuss or write about their comparisons.

Other Activities

- Theme 1 Assignment Cards 7, 8, 9
- TE p. 100, Literature Discussion
- TE p. 107, Social Studies
- TE p. 107E, Challenge Word Practice

- TE pp. R13, R21, Challenge
- Education Place: www.eduplace.com More activities related to *Finding the* Titanic
- Accelerated Reader®, *Finding the* Titanic

2

Expected Outcome

A good essay will include

✓ a well-organized argument that shows a relationship among ideas

✓ references to story details that support the student's reasoning

✓ persuasive language

3

Expected Outcome

A good diorama will include

✓ a well-planned execution of the task

✓ resourceful use of materials

✓ reflection of the details in the selection

Challenge Master CH 1–6

THEME 1 / *Finding the* Titanic

Name_____

2. To Preserve or Not to Preserve?

Goal: Write a persuasive essay about whether the *Titanic* should be left undisturbed as a monument or not.

- Support your opinion with strong reasons that appeal to your audience.
- Support your reasons with facts and examples.
- Answer any objections you think your audience might have.
- Order your reasons from least to most important.
- Use positive, confident language.
- End by summing up your reasons and repeating your opinion.

TIPS
- Draft your essay with a strong introduction.
- Use details to explain each reason.

3. Diorama

Goal: Create a diorama of what Robert Ballard and his crew found two and one-half miles down on the bottom of the Atlantic Ocean.

Reread *Finding the* Titanic and make notes about what Robert Ballard found. Think about

- what materials you might work with
- whether to use models, pictures, or realistic materials
- how large to make your diorama
- what kind of explanatory material, if any, to include

TIPS
- Use graph paper to plan your diorama.
- Refer to reference sources for photographs and background data.

Grade 4 Theme 1: Journeys   Challenge Master CH 1–6

Activities

Challenge Master CH 1–7

THEME 1/*By the Shores of Silver Lake*

Name _____

1. A Sense-ible Source Book

Goal: Create a source book of the senses.

Brainstorm Topics

First, freely list sense words that come to mind. Include

• images and textures

• words, synonyms, definitions

• examples from magazines, books, television, and other sources

Jot down any other words that come to mind. Then organize your words into categories representing the five senses.

Create the Pages

Using your categorized word lists, make a table of contents for your book.

• Write the sense category, for example, *Sight*, and any words you brainstormed for that category.

• Create a book page for each sense word.

• Include a picture to represent each word.

TIPS

• Be sure that your words are categorized under the right sense.

• Include many descriptive words and images.

Put Your Book Together

Assemble your pages in a book or loose-leaf binder.

• Place your table of contents in the front. Arrange your pages in the order of the table of contents.

• Create an interesting cover that relates to the subject.

CH 1–7 Challenge Master   Grade 4 Theme 1: Journeys

Copyright © Houghton Mifflin Company. All rights reserved.

---

①

Expected Outcome

A good source book will include

✔ words that represent each of the five senses

✔ book pages categorized under the appropriate sense

✔ descriptive words and images

---

1. A Sense-ible Source Book

<u>150 MINUTES</u>   INDIVIDUAL   SMALL GROUP

(Science)

Materials: crayons, markers, drawing paper, old magazines and a loose-leaf binder (optional)

DAY 1

Brainstorm Topics

Have students reread pages 121–123 of *By the Shores of Silver Lake* and notice how Laura "sees out loud" for Mary. Laura's descriptive words created a picture that Mary could see in her mind. Have students keep in mind how descriptive words can represent the senses as they brainstorm their words.

English Language Learners: Have students share some sense words from their primary languages.

DAY 2

Students continue to work on this project.

DAY 3

Create the Pages

Check with students on the progress of their tables of contents and book pages.

DAY 4

Students continue to work on this project.

DAY 5

Put Your Book Together

If more than one student has worked on this activity, you may wish to have them combine their efforts. You might ask the school librarian if he or she would like a copy of the book for the library.

---

2. The First Time I Ever . . .

60 MINUTES   INDIVIDUAL

Before they begin writing, have students brainstorm several ideas before they narrow down the list to one best suited to this type of essay. Remind them to

- add important details that provide story structure
- add interest, humor, or suspense to the essay

3. Seeing Out Loud   60 MINUTES   INDIVIDUAL

Materials: drawing paper, crayons, and markers

Tell students to

- visualize the entire scene
- sketch it lightly

You may wish to have several students draw while one narrates, then compare and contrast their work.

Additional Independent Work
Connecting/Comparing Literature

Have students compare the Leveled Reader selection *Prairie Danger* with the anthology selection *By the Shores of Silver Lake,* using what they have learned about Noting Details. Students may discuss or write about their comparisons.

Other Activities

- Theme 1 Assignment Cards 10, 11, 12
- TE p. 126, Literature Discussion
- TE p. 133, Word Study
- TE p. 133E, Challenge Word Practice

- TE pp. R15, R23, Challenge
- Education Place: www.eduplace.com More activities related to *By the Shores of Silver Lake*
- Accelerated Reader®, *By the Shores of Silver Lake*

Expected Outcome

A good essay will include

✔ details that add color to the essay

✔ clear writing

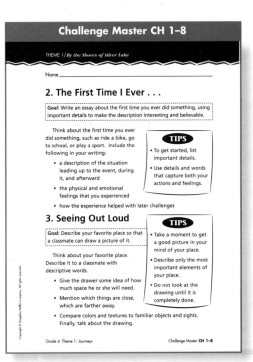

Expected Outcome

A good drawing will include

✔ the most important elements described by the speaker

✔ a sense of order that organizes diverse elements

Theme 2

CHALLENGE ACTIVITIES FOR

American Stories

Selections

1 Tomás and
the Library Lady

2 Tanya's Reunion

3 Boss of the Plains

4 A Very Important Day

Activities

Challenge Master CH 2-1

THEME 2/*Tomás and the Library Lady*

Name _____

1. The Library, Live!

Goal: Create interest in a favorite library book by giving a dramatic presentation based on it.

Choose Your Inspiration

When you finish a book you really enjoy, do you tell others about it? Do you wish there were more of it?

- Jot down the names of three library books you have enjoyed, and list things that appealed to you.
- Choose one book to present to your classmates.

Choose Your Scene

Look through the book to

- find passages that show the qualities you like most
- choose a passage that is simple enough to act out
- think how to adapt the passage

You may decide on a monologue, a retelling from one point of view.

TIPS
- Choose a passage that is exciting and will catch your audience's attention.
- Practice in front of a mirror and with a helpful friend.

Show What You Know

Think about how you can present your passage so that it appeals to your audience. Choose one of these ideas or an idea of your own.

- Make stick puppets of a major character or characters to hold up as you act out part of the story.
- Dress up as one character in a simple costume.

CH **2-1** Challenge Master   Grade 4 Theme 2: American Stories

Copyright © Houghton Mifflin Company. All rights reserved.

1

Expected Outcome

A good presentation will include

✔ an excerpt that demonstrates the qualities of the book, such as how the story is told, the exciting events, the characters, and so forth

✔ a well-rehearsed, well-planned, and creative presentation

---

1. The Library, Live! ⎸50 MINUTES INDIVIDUAL

Materials: *stiff paper, cardboard, or oak tag; ice cream sticks or others; and miscellaneous clean, recycled scraps*

DAY 1

Choose Your Inspiration

Tell students that they should think carefully about the qualities of the book that they like. Offer the following guidelines:

- Choose a book whose special qualities you can identify easily. Think about the characters, the setting, how the story is told, exciting events, and so forth.
- As an option, look for a character with a strong personality whose "voice" can carry the story.

English Language Learners: Brainstorm with students lists of qualities of their favorite characters.

DAY 2

Students continue to work on this project.

DAY 3

Choose Your Scene

Check with students on their progress in choosing a book and a passage to present. Remind them that their goals are to generate interest and curiosity in a book.

DAY 4

Students continue to work on this project.

DAY 5

Show What You Know

- Tell students to choose a presentation format that showcases the main qualities of their story and will interest their audience.
- Invite other classes to watch the presentations.

2. Meet the Librarian 60 MINUTES INDIVIDUAL

Materials: tape recorder (optional)

If more than one student works on this activity, suggest a group interview in which interviewers pool their questions but prepare their own articles from their notes.

3. From Seedling to Harvest

60 MINUTES INDIVIDUAL

(Social Studies) (Science)

Materials: diagram of the life cycle of a major crop

Remind students to clarify when work is done by people rather than machines. If necessary, review sequence of events and time words with students.

Additional Independent Work
Connecting/Comparing Literature

Have students compare the Leveled Reader selection *Emma Rides on the Erie Canal* with the anthology selection *Tomás and the Library Lady,* using what they have learned about sequence of events. Students may discuss or write about their comparisons.

Other Activities

- Theme 2 Assignment Cards 1, 2
- TE p. 174, Literature Discussion
- TE p. 181, Social Studies
- TE p. 181E, Challenge Word Practice

- TE pp. R9, R17, Challenge
- Education Place: www.eduplace.com More activities related to *Tomás and the Library Lady*
- Accelerated Reader®, *Tomás and the Library Lady*

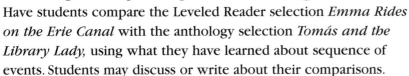

2 Expected Outcome

A good interview will include

✔ the date and time of the interview, details and information that answer student interview questions

✔ paraphrased answers and direct quotations from the librarian

✔ a well-organized summary with a strong opening and effective closing

3 Expected Outcome

A good story will include

✔ specific details of the life cycle of a crop grown in Texas or Iowa

✔ a clear description of how the work is done

✔ an orderly presentation of a sequence of events

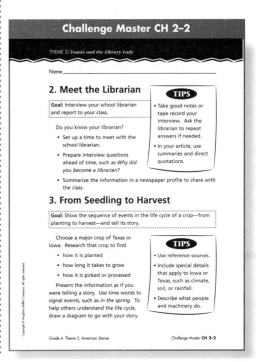

Activities

Challenge Master CH 2–3

THEME 2/*Tanya's Reunion*

Name _____

1. Road Games

Goal: Publish a book of family games to play on a trip.

Collecting

There are many games that people have invented over the years to make traveling more fun. You can collect your favorites into a book.

• Ask family members and friends for suggestions of games that help pass the time on a long trip.

• Add games or puzzles that you've enjoyed.

• Make notes about each game and how to play it.

Sorting Out

List the kinds of games you want in your book such as games that

• are for all ages

• aren't too noisy

• don't need any special equipment

• might be for only one player

Choose at least ten games that match your list.

TIPS

• Start out with more than ten ideas so you have many to choose from. Remember to title each game.

• Write clear directions and find or draw helpful illustrations.

• Group the same kind of games together.

Show What You Know

Turn your list into a book. You may want to use a computer to type the pages and make the pictures. Decide how to publish your information.

CH 2–3 Challenge Master   Grade 4 Theme 2: American Stories

Copyright © Houghton Mifflin Company. All rights reserved.

❶ Expected Outcome

A good handbook will include

✔ clear presentation and a title for each game

✔ easy-to-follow directions

✔ a readable format with helpful illustrations

1. Road Games   <u>60 MINUTES</u>   INDIVIDUAL

Materials: *game books, a hole punch, index cards, folders, drawing paper, crayons, and markers*

DAY 1

Collecting

Explain that it can be hard to read a lot of text in a moving vehicle. Therefore, the games should not require much reading. Games could include things passengers can see out the windows, such as

• buildings

• license plates

• road and other signs

Remind students to check their notes and carefully explain how to play each game.

DAY 2

Students continue to work on this project.

DAY 3

Sorting Out

Check with students on the progress of their books. Tell them that their list will help them to include games they want.

English Language Learners: Students might like to make a game book with directions in their primary language and in English.

DAY 4

Students continue to work on this project.

DAY 5

Show What You Know

Each student should proofread his or her work. If possible, make duplicates for each student to take home.

2. *In Search of the Grand Canyon*

60 MINUTES   INDIVIDUAL   PAIR

(Challenge Theme Paperback)

(Science)

Materials: a dictionary and tracing paper

Students should make their choices after reviewing the text for more than one event.

3. A Quality Character 60 MINUTES   INDIVIDUAL

Advise students that they need factual material to support their opinions. Ask volunteers to share their character sketches with the class.

Additional Independent Work
Connecting/Comparing Literature

Have students compare the Leveled Reader selection *Coming Home* with the anthology selection *Tanya's Reunion,* using what they have learned about Making Inferences. Students may discuss or write about their comparisons.

Other Activities

- Challenge Theme Paperback, *In Search of the Grand Canyon*
- Theme 2 Assignment Cards 3, 4
- TE p. 210, Literature Discussion
- TE p. 215E, Challenge Word Practice

- TE pp. R6, R11, R19, Challenge
- Education Place: www.eduplace.com More activities related to *Tanya's Reunion*
- Accelerated Reader®, *Tanya's Reunion*

---

❷

Expected Outcome

A good report will include

✔ important events from the text

✔ details that bring the events to life

---

❸

Expected Outcome

A good character sketch will include

✔ factual material

✔ references to the writer's own life experiences

✔ realistic inferences based on facts

Challenge Master CH 2–4

THEME 2/*Tanya's Reunion*

Name _____

2. *In Search of the Grand Canyon*

Goal: Write a report that John Wesley Powell might have written about his journey in *In Search of the Grand Canyon.*

The book *In Search of the Grand Canyon* tells of a thrilling and sometimes dangerous trip. Choose two moments when Powell and his companions saw unfamiliar things and gave them new names. Write a report about those moments.

- Explain where Powell and his companions were and show it on a map of the Grand Canyon.
- Describe, in your own words, what happened.
- Tell what the new names were and why the men chose them.

TIPS
- Present the facts in order.
- Include descriptive words and phrases.

3. A Quality Character

Goal: Write a character sketch of a person whom you admire.

- Choose a person. If necessary, research that person's life.
- Write a short character sketch of that person.

Make an inference chart that shows
- the events or facts you describe in your sketch

TIPS
- Get your information from a dependable source.
- Base your inferences on facts, not on opinions.

- references to similar events or facts from your life
- the inferences you made based on the person's qualities

Grade 4 Theme 2: American Stories

Challenge Master **CH 2–4**

Activities

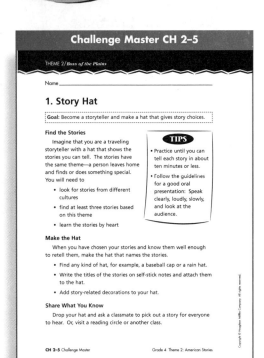

Challenge Master CH 2–5

THEME 2/ *Boss of the Plains*

Name

1. Story Hat

Goal: Become a storyteller and make a hat that gives story choices.

Find the Stories

Imagine that you are a traveling storyteller with a hat that shows the stories you can tell. The stories have the same theme—a person leaves home and finds or does something special. You will need to

• look for stories from different cultures

• find at least three stories based on this theme

• learn the stories by heart

TIPS

• Practice until you can tell each story in about ten minutes or less.

• Follow the guidelines for a good oral presentation: Speak clearly, loudly, slowly, and look at the audience.

Make the Hat

When you have chosen your stories and know them well enough to retell them, make the hat that names the stories.

• Find any kind of hat, for example, a baseball cap or a rain hat.

• Write the titles of the stories on self-stick notes and attach them to the hat.

• Add story-related decorations to your hat.

Share What You Know

Drop your hat and ask a classmate to pick out a story for everyone to hear. Or, visit a reading circle or another class.

CH 2–5 Challenge Master   Grade 4 Theme 2: American Stories

①

Expected Outcome

Good storytelling will include

✔ stories that have the same theme but represent different cultures

✔ decorated hat

✔ practiced and fluent oral presentation lasting about thirty minutes

1. Story Hat   150 MINUTES   INDIVIDUAL   PAIR   SMALL GROUP

(Social Studies)

Materials: self-stick notes, tape or glue, construction paper, crayons, markers, and anthologies of traditional stories

DAY 1

Find the Stories

Tell students of the tradition of oral storytelling. Explain how traveling storytellers used their storytelling to earn a living and by chance to spread the culture of their people. Then suggest that students use these guidelines in selecting stories:

• Choose simple stories.

• Choose stories that make it clear what the main character is seeking.

• Choose stories that reflect their original culture.

Students read and select three stories. Students practice retelling the selected stories.

English Language Learners: Students may be able to share stories from their primary language. Have beginners work with more advanced students to present the story in English.

DAY 2

Students continue to work on this project.

DAY 3

Make the Hat

Check with students on the progress of their story gathering.

• Have them time their stories for ten minutes or less.

• Allow time for rehearsal and, if possible, an audio recording.

• For health reasons, participants should not share hats.

DAY 4

Students continue to work on this project.

DAY 5

Share What You Know

• The storytellers should introduce themselves and say whether the audience is to take part.

• You may wish to let the storytellers surprise their audiences. Or a "runner" can announce the storytellers' approach.

2. What's the Reason? *60 MINUTES* INDIVIDUAL PAIR
(Social Studies)

Materials: reference sources

Students may make different generalizations based on the same facts. Discuss how the same facts can be interpreted in different ways. Remind students that their generalizations should include signal words like *most, often,* and *usually.*

3. Song of the West *60 MINUTES* INDIVIDUAL PAIR
(Social Studies) (Music)

Materials: songbooks or recordings of traditional tunes

Tell students that in writing lyrics their main concerns should be

- to capture the rhythm, mood, and special vocabulary of the work.
- to fit the lyrics to the music.

English Language Learners: Students might use tunes from their primary language.

Additional Independent Work
Connecting/Comparing Literature

Have students compare the Leveled Reader selection *Elisha Otis's Ups and Downs* with the anthology selection *Boss of the Plains,* using what they have learned about Making Generalizations. Students may discuss or write about their comparisons.

Other Activities

- Theme 2 Assignment Cards 5, 6, 7
- TE p. 238, Literature Discussion
- TE p. 245, Music
- TE p. 245E, Challenge Word Practice

- TE pp. R13, R21, Challenge
- Education Place: www.eduplace.com More activities related to *Boss of the Plains*
- Accelerated Reader®, *Boss of the Plains*

Expected Outcome

A good result will include

✔ three acceptable generalizations as to why people wear hats

✔ a well-organized chart showing the bases for the generalizations

✔ words that signal a generalization, such as *often, few, many,* and so forth

Expected Outcome

A good song will include

✔ a familiar tune

✔ lyrics that match the tune

✔ lyrics that tell something about the work

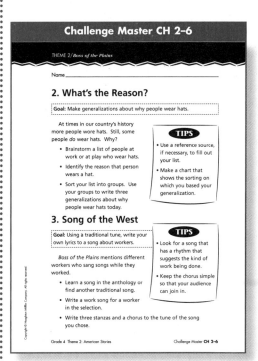

Challenge Master CH 2-6

THEME 2/*Boss of the Plains*

Name_____

2. What's the Reason?

Goal: Make generalizations about why people wear hats.

At times in our country's history more people wore hats. Still, some people do wear hats. Why?

- Brainstorm a list of people at work or at play who wear hats.
- Identify the reason that person wears a hat.
- Sort your list into groups. Use your groups to write three generalizations about why people wear hats today.

TIPS
- Use a reference source, if necessary, to fill out your list.
- Make a chart that shows the sorting on which you based your generalization.

3. Song of the West

Goal: Using a traditional tune, write your own lyrics to a song about workers.

Boss of the Plains mentions different workers who sang songs while they worked.

- Learn a song in the anthology or find another traditional song.
- Write a work song for a worker in the selection.
- Write three stanzas and a chorus to the tune of the song you chose.

TIPS
- Look for a song that has a rhythm that suggests the kind of work being done.
- Keep the chorus simple so that your audience can join in.

Grade 4 Theme 2: American Stories

Challenge Master **CH 2-6**

Challenge Master CH 2–7

THEME 2/*A Very Important Day*

Name _____

1. The Start of a New Day

Goal: Suggest a new holiday the democratic way.

Set Up the Choices

What if you could create a new holiday? Use the following steps:

• Form a holiday committee.

• As a group select a moderator to run the meeting, a secretary to take notes, and a recorder to count votes.

• Each committee member will list ideas about what the holiday will honor, its name, and when it will be celebrated.

Vote on the Holiday

Meet again to narrow the choices and discuss favorite ideas. Decide on three of the suggested holidays to put on a ballot. The ballot should have a yes/no format. Distribute the ballots to committee members and hold a vote. The suggestion with the most votes may become the new holiday.

TIPS

• Have the moderator set time limits so that every committee member can take part.

• Write a draft version of the decision so that committee members can review it before presenting it to the class.

Share What You Know

Create a poster that announces the new holiday. It should

• name the new holiday

• describe its purpose

• declare how it ought to be celebrated

Present your new holiday to the class.

CH 2–7 Challenge Master   Grade 4 Theme 2: American Stories

---

① Expected Outcome

A new holiday will include

✔ evidence that it is the product of a democratic process

✔ posters with clear language in a well-organized format

✔ innovative ideas

---

1. The Start of a New Day

150 MINUTES   SMALL GROUP

Materials: poster board, crayons, markers, and a calendar showing all current holidays

DAY 1

Set Up the Choices

Have students form small groups. Ask if they know the guidelines for a democratic procedure, including

• raising one's hand for recognition from the moderator

• listening carefully as others speak

• not interrupting other speakers

Students may wish to make and illustrate a poster with guidelines for a democratic procedure.

English Language Learners: Group students with fluent speakers or students with a more advanced facility with the language.

DAY 2

Students continue to work on this project.

DAY 3

Vote on the Holiday

Check on the progress of the choices and the ballot. Explain what a majority vote is.

DAY 4

Students continue to work on this project.

DAY 5

Share What You Know

If more than one group has created a holiday, you may wish to have the entire class vote their preference. If possible, arrange to observe the created holiday in your classroom.

2. New Americans' Contributions

<u>60 MINUTES</u>   INDIVIDUAL

Materials: *encyclopedia and other reference sources*

You might want to brainstorm a list of famous immigrants. Remind students that an immigrant is anyone from another country who comes to the United States to live permanently.

3. Sorting States   <u>60 MINUTES</u>   INDIVIDUAL   PAIR
(Social Studies)

Materials: *map of the United States*

Point out that there are many categories to choose from. Be sure that every state belongs in its chosen category.

Additional Independent Work
Connecting/Comparing Literature

Have students compare the Leveled Reader selection *Poppy's Timeline* with the anthology selection *A Very Important Day,* using what they have learned about Categorize and Classify. Students may discuss or write about their comparisons.

Other Activities

- Theme 2 Assignment Cards 8, 9, 10
- TE p. 268, Literature Discussion
- TE p. 275, Mock Election
- TE p. 275E, Challenge Word Practice

- TE pp. R15, R23, Challenge
- Education Place: www.eduplace.com More activities related to *A Very Important Day*
- Accelerated Reader®, *A Very Important Day*

2

Expected Outcome

A good report will include

✓ a clear presentation of facts

✓ the major contributions of the chosen person

✓ why that person was chosen

3

Expected Outcome

A good word web will include

✓ clearly understandable categories

✓ states that belong in each category

✓ an organized format

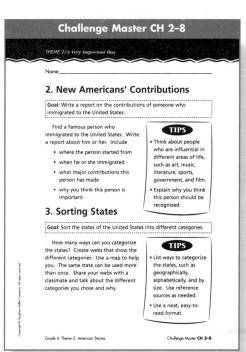

Challenge Master CH 2–8

THEME 2/*A Very Important Day*

Name _____

2. New Americans' Contributions

Goal: Write a report on the contributions of someone who immigrated to the United States.

Find a famous person who immigrated to the United States. Write a report about him or her. Include

- where the person started from
- when he or she immigrated
- what major contributions this person has made
- why you think this person is important

TIPS

- Think about people who are influential in different areas of life, such as art, music, literature, sports, government, and film.
- Explain why you think this person should be recognized.

3. Sorting States

Goal: Sort the states of the United States into different categories.

How many ways can you categorize the states? Create webs that show the different categories. Use a map to help you. The same state can be used more than once. Share your webs with a classmate and talk about the different categories you chose and why.

TIPS

- List ways to categorize the states, such as geographically, alphabetically, and by size. Use reference sources as needed.
- Use a neat, easy-to-read format.

Grade 4 Theme 2: American Stories   Challenge Master **CH 2–8**

Copyright © Houghton Mifflin Company. All rights reserved.

Theme 3

That's Amazing!

Selections

1 The Stranger

2 Cendrillon

3 Heat Wave!

Activities

Challenge Master CH 3-1

THEME 3/*The Stranger*

Name _____

1. Showing Change Over Time

Goal: Show a change in nature as it occurs over time.

Find the Facts

When leaves change color in the fall, it happens over a period of time. Find an example in nature of this kind of change. Some suggestions:

- the development of a bird from egg to flight
- a plant from seed to flower or to fruit
- a tadpole changing into a frog

Take detailed notes on your research. Write down your reference sources. Check your completed work against them.

Organize and Present the Facts

Think what you might show visually. Decide what you will explain in text.

Choose one of these ideas or an idea of your own:

- a filmstrip (on a roll of paper)
- a series of strips explaining the stages of development
- an illustrated, step-by-step diagram or flowchart

TIPS
- Label important details of visual aids.
- Write text that helps the class connect the steps.
- Present your information logically.

Share What You Know

Give an oral presentation to the class. Provide handouts or models. Have a question-and-answer session.

CH 3-1 Challenge Master   Grade 4 Theme 3: That's Amazing!

Copyright © Houghton Mifflin Company. All rights reserved.

---

❶ Expected Outcome

A good presentation will include

✔ labeled visual aids and clear text

✔ a connection between steps

✔ logically presented information

---

1. Showing Change Over Time

150 MINUTES   INDIVIDUAL

(Science)

Materials: *reference source, drawing paper, crayons, markers, paper in a roll, tape, stapler, and recycled materials, such as cardboard rolls*

DAY 1

Find the Facts

Have students do the following:

- Become familiar with reference sources.
- Decide to show all or just part of a process of change.
- Make the visual aids accurate.
- Write descriptive text.

English Language Learners: Guide students to well-illustrated resources with fairly easy text.

DAY 2

Students continue to work on this project.

DAY 3

Organize and Present the Facts

Check with students on the progress of their presentation.

- Remind students that their goal is to show change in nature. Their choice of material should reflect the process and major stages.
- Students may have chosen a process of change that is too complex or too lengthy; they will need to trim their project.

DAY 4

Students continue to work on this project.

DAY 5

Share What You Know

Provide a space where students can present their work and display it for others to examine. You might want to moderate the question-and-answer session.

2. Synonym Dominoes

60 MINUTES   INDIVIDUAL   PAIR

Materials: unlined index cards, thesaurus (optional)

You might want to review dominoes with students. For an extra challenge, have students create antonym dominoes.

3. Drawing Word Pictures

60 MINUTES   INDIVIDUAL

Materials: encyclopedia, books on trees, drawing paper, and markers

Students should use their own observation and eye for details to complete the word picture of a particular tree. You might display word pictures on a classroom bulletin board.

Additional Independent Work

Connecting/Comparing Literature ⭐

Have students compare the Leveled Reader selection *Wings for a Day* with the anthology selection *The Stranger,* using what they have learned about Noting Details. Students may discuss or write about their comparisons.

Other Activities

- Theme 3 Assignment Cards 1, 2, 3
- TE p. 316, Literature Discussion
- TE p. 322, Writing
- TE p. 323E, Challenge Word Practice

- TE pp. R9, R15, Challenge
- Education Place: www.eduplace.com More activities related to *The Stranger*
- Accelerated Reader®, *The Stranger*

Expected Outcome

A good game will include

- ✔ 20 pairs of synonyms and four nonrelated words
- ✔ a smooth flow of play
- ✔ neatly printed words on cards

Expected Outcome

A good word picture will include

- ✔ details of shape, size, color, and texture and seasonal features such as leaves, flowers, and fruit
- ✔ details sorted into categories according to parts of the tree
- ✔ words and details in the shape of a tree

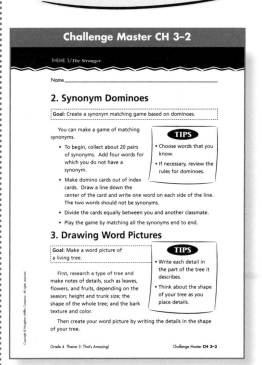

Challenge Master CH 3–2

THEME 3/*The Stranger*

Name_____

2. Synonym Dominoes

Goal: Create a synonym matching game based on dominoes.

You can make a game of matching synonyms.

- To begin, collect about 20 pairs of synonyms. Add four words for which you do not have a synonym.
- Make domino cards out of index cards. Draw a line down the center of the card and write one word on each side of the line. The two words should not be synonyms.
- Divide the cards equally between you and another classmate.
- Play the game by matching all the synonyms end to end.

TIPS
- Choose words that you know.
- If necessary, review the rules for dominoes.

3. Drawing Word Pictures

Goal: Make a word picture of a living tree.

First, research a type of tree and make notes of details, such as leaves, flowers, and fruits, depending on the season; height and trunk size; the shape of the whole tree; and the bark texture and color.

Then create your word picture by writing the details in the shape of your tree.

TIPS
- Write each detail in the part of the tree it describes.
- Think about the shape of your tree as you place details.

Grade 4 Theme 3: That's Amazing!   Challenge Master **CH 3-2**

SELECTION 1: *The Stranger* (23)

Challenge Master CH 3-3

THEME 3/*Cendrillon*

Name _____

1. What Really Happened?

Goal: Retell the story *Cendrillon* from different perspectives.

Revisit the Story
- Interview the other main characters in *Cendrillon* to get their versions of events.
- Make one list of questions to ask the characters.
- Each version of the story should have the same events, but will be different depending on each character's point of view.

Compare the Versions
Collect all the versions and put them together to retell the story.
- Make notes for the new version from each interview.
- List all the events in the story.
- Match each event with the character you've picked to tell about it.
- Include something from the point of view of everyone you interview.
- Include the same plot elements that occur in *Cendrillon*.

Share What You Know
Decide how to retell and present your story to the class. You might:
- Present your new story orally.
- Act out your retelling by role-playing the different characters.
- Write and illustrate your version.

TIPS
- Reread the story.
- Make a list of the main characters to be sure to interview them all.
- Choose a presentation that will include all the elements of your story.

CH 3-3 Challenge Master   Grade 4 Theme 3: That's Amazing!

Copyright © Houghton Mifflin Company. All rights reserved.

①

Expected Outcome

A good retelling will include

✔ interviews of the main characters

✔ a creative and well-planned presentation that includes all elements of the story

1. What Really Happened?

150 MINUTES   INDIVIDUAL

DAY 1

Revisit the Story

Make it clear to students that their presentation is to be a work of imagination. To make their presentation convincing, they should

- think carefully about the characters' thoughts and feelings.
- make any changes from the original plot consistent with each character's personality.

List possible plot changes, and assign each change to a different character.

English Language Learners: Present the activity as a form of role-playing in which characters step out of the story and speak for themselves.

DAY 2

Students continue to work on this project.

DAY 3

Compare the Versions

Check with students on the progress of their retellings.

- Remind students that each character has a different point of view.
- Tell students to include every main character in their retelling.

DAY 4

Students continue to work on this project.

DAY 5

Share What You Know

Give students time to prepare their presentations. Tell students to consider a format that showcases the imaginative element in their work. Invite other classes to come to the retellings.

2. *The Real Thief* 60 MINUTES INDIVIDUAL PAIR
(Challenge Theme Paperback)

Have students create a before-and-after chart to help them analyze Gawain's character. Explain the terms *static* and *dynamic.* Tell students that *static* characters do not change, but *dynamic* characters do. Discuss with students how Gawain is a *dynamic* character.

3. Island Life 60 MINUTES INDIVIDUAL
(Social Studies)

Materials: reference sources, almanacs, atlas, and encyclopedia

If necessary, review comparing and contrasting with students. You may wish to review with students which two islands each has chosen before they begin this activity.

Additional Independent Work
Connecting/Comparing Literature

Have students compare the Leveled Reader selection *Juan's Three Wishes* with the anthology selection *Cendrillon,* using what they have learned about Compare and Contrast. Students may discuss or write about their comparisons.

Other Activities

- Challenge Theme Paperback, *The Real Thief*
- Theme 3 Assignment Cards 4, 5, 6
- TE p. 332, Storytelling Style
- TE p. 352, Literature Discussion
- TE p. 357E, Challenge Word Practice

- TE pp. R6, R11, R17, Challenge
- Education Place: www.eduplace.com More activities related to *Cendrillon*
- Accelerated Reader®, *Cendrillon*

2

Expected Outcome

A good character sketch will include

✔ Gawain's character traits

✔ references to actions that illustrate each trait

✔ an understanding of the relationship between events in the story and the change in Gawain's character

3

Expected Outcome

A good chart will include

✔ accurate details about each island

✔ similarities and differences in the way of life on the two islands

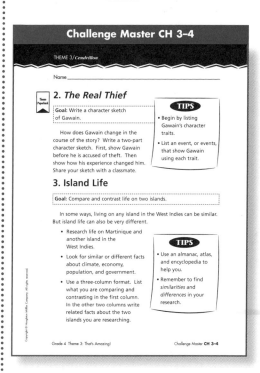

Activities

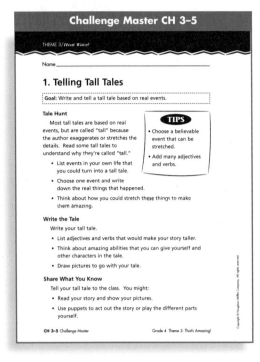

Challenge Master CH 3–5

THEME 3/*Heat Wave!*

Name _____

1. Telling Tall Tales

Goal: Write and tell a tall tale based on real events.

Tale Hunt

Most tall tales are based on real events, but are called "tall" because the author exaggerates or stretches the details. Read some tall tales to understand why they're called "tall."

TIPS

• Choose a believable event that can be stretched.
• Add many adjectives and verbs.

• List events in your own life that you could turn into a tall tale.
• Choose one event and write down the real things that happened.
• Think about how you could stretch these things to make them amazing.

Write the Tale

Write your tall tale.

• List adjectives and verbs that would make your story taller.
• Think about amazing abilities that you can give yourself and other characters in the tale.
• Draw pictures to go with your tale.

Share What You Know

Tell your tall tale to the class. You might:

• Read your story and show your pictures.
• Use puppets to act out the story or play the different parts yourself.

CH 3–5 Challenge Master   Grade 4 Theme 3: That's Amazing!

Copyright © Houghton Mifflin Company. All rights reserved.

1

Expected Outcome

A good tall tale will include

✔ a believable event as a base

✔ exaggerated elements

✔ a clearly delivered presentation

1. Telling Tall Tales 150 MINUTES INDIVIDUAL

Materials: *anthologies of tall tales, drawing paper, markers, and crayons*

DAY 1

Tale Hunt

Ask students to list some tall tales and note exaggerated elements that make them "tall." Remind students to choose an event that is easily stretched. Have students brainstorm adjectives and verbs.

Students should continue to read tall tales and to think of ways to exaggerate real events.

English Language Learners: Review the concept of tall tales and exaggeration with students.

DAY 2

Students continue to work on this project.

DAY 3

Write the Tale

Have students create a chart of what might happen in their chosen event. Have them list ideas to make their tall tale truly amazing. Students should illustrate their tales.

DAY 4

Students continue to work on this project.

DAY 5

Share What You Know

Provide rehearsal time so that students can perform confidently before the class. If possible, invite other classes to hear the tales.

2. Fact or Fantasy? <u>60 MINUTES</u> INDIVIDUAL
(Science)

Materials: reference sources

Tell students that a saying might sometimes be true but is not always true. A scientific fact, however, will be true every time.

3. Ms. Incredible <u>60 MINUTES</u> INDIVIDUAL
Materials: drawing paper, crayons, and markers

Have students think about what it would be like to be an amazing athlete; then use that as a basis for their stories. They should think of their story as a wish come true.

Additional Independent Work
Connecting/Comparing Literature

Have students compare the Leveled Reader selection *Sluefoot Sue's Wild Ride* with the anthology selection *Heat Wave!*, using what they have learned about Fantasy and Realism. Students may discuss or write about their comparisons.

Other Activities

- Theme 3 Assignment Cards 7, 8, 9
- TE p. 376, Literature Discussion
- TE p. 381, Math
- TE p. 381E, Challenge Word Practice

- TE pp. R13, R19, Challenge
- Education Place: www.eduplace.com More activities related to *Heat Wave!*
- Accelerated Reader®, *Heat Wave!*

Expected Outcome
A good activity will include
- ✔ evidence for accepting or rejecting the saying as fact
- ✔ an accurate source list
- ✔ well-organized material

Expected Outcome
A good newspaper story will include
- ✔ an interesting character
- ✔ realistic details about the sport and amazing details about the skill
- ✔ an illustration of the athlete practicing the skill

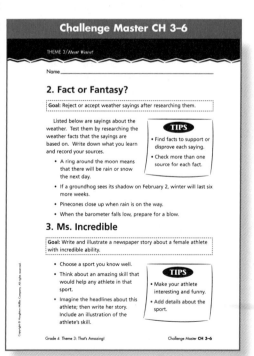

Theme 4

Problem Solvers

Selections

Activities

Challenge Master CH 4–1

THEME 4/ *My Name Is María Isabel*

Name_____

1. Problem-Solving Skit

Goal: Write and perform a skit in which characters identify and solve a problem.

TIPS
- Choose a problem that has a clear solution.
- When writing the skit, follow a story structure.

Decide on the Problem

With a small group of classmates brainstorm a list of problems the characters in your skit could solve. Think about

- problems you have solved
- problems in which you overcame obstacles to reach a goal
- problems that would be interesting to your audience

Choose one problem from your list for your skit. Think about a way to act out this problem and its solution.

Write Your Skit

Write a short script for your skit. Think about

- how many characters you need so that every member of the group participates
- what each character will say
- what part each character will have in solving the problem

Assign a character to each member of your group. Practice your skit together. Make any necessary changes to improve it.

Share What You Know

Once you feel comfortable with your skit, perform it for the class. Speak clearly so that everyone can hear you. Ask the class if they can tell you what the problem was and how the characters solved it.

CH 4–1 Challenge Master   Grade 4 Theme 4: Problem Solvers

Copyright © Houghton Mifflin Company. All rights reserved.

Expected Outcome

A good skit will include

✔ a clear problem and solution

✔ well-written dialogue

✔ participation by everyone in the group

1. Problem-Solving Skit

150 MINUTES   SMALL GROUP

DAY 1

Decide on the Problem

Tell students that each member of the group should contribute at least one problem and solution to the list. Refer students to page 1 of the Practice Book to help them come up with ideas.

English Language Learners: You might want to review the terms *problem* and *solution* with students. Pair students with primary English speakers or students with a more advanced facility with the language.

DAY 2

Write Your Skit

Tell students that their skit should stick to the problem as the main topic and that their dialogue should relate to the problem or solution.

DAY 3

Check with students on the progress of their skit.

DAY 4

Allow students enough time to practice and revise their skit.

DAY 5

Share What You Know

You might want to mediate the discussion about the skit between the group and the audience. Invite other classes to watch the skit.

2. Go, Team, Go! 60 MINUTES   INDIVIDUAL

Materials: *sports pages (optional) and sports almanac (optional)*

Point out that students' predictions should be backed up by evidence such as recent statistics and/or an analysis of a player's or team's potential.

3. Alternative Solutions 60 MINUTES   INDIVIDUAL

Remind students to focus their efforts on a solution that is entertaining and workable. You might want to have students share their alternative endings with the class.

Additional Independent Work
Connecting/Comparing Literature

Have students compare the Leveled Reader selection *The Right Fly* with the anthology selection *My Name Is María Isabel,* using what they have learned about Predicting Outcomes. Students may discuss or write about their comparisons.

Other Activities

- Theme 4 Assignment Cards 1, 2, 3, 4
- TE p. 406, Literature Discussion
- TE p. 411, What's in a Name?
- TE p. 411E, Challenge Word Practice

- TE pp. R9, R17, Challenge
- Education Place: www.eduplace.com
  More activities related to *My Name Is María Isabel*
- Accelerated Reader®, *My Name Is María Isabel*

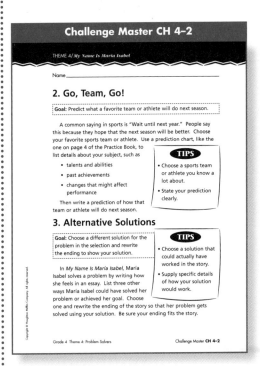

2

Expected Outcome

A good prediction will include

✔ a clearly stated theory

✔ details that support the theory

✔ a well-reasoned argument

3

Expected Outcome

A good rewrite will

✔ be consistent with details from the story

✔ follow the story's point of view

✔ present a clear and workable solution

Challenge Master CH 4–2

THEME 4/*My Name Is María Isabel*

Name _____

2. Go, Team, Go!

Goal: Predict what a favorite team or athlete will do next season.

A common saying in sports is "Wait until next year." People say this because they hope that the next season will be better. Choose your favorite sports team or athlete. Use a prediction chart, like the one on page 4 of the Practice Book, to list details about your subject, such as

- talents and abilities
- past achievements
- changes that might affect performance

Then write a prediction of how that team or athlete will do next season.

TIPS
- Choose a sports team or athlete you know a lot about.
- State your prediction clearly.

3. Alternative Solutions

Goal: Choose a different solution for the problem in the selection and rewrite the ending to show your solution.

In *My Name Is María Isabel,* María Isabel solves a problem by writing how she feels in an essay. List three other ways María Isabel could have solved her problem or achieved her goal. Choose one and rewrite the ending of the story so that her problem gets solved using your solution. Be sure your ending fits the story.

TIPS
- Choose a solution that could actually have worked in the story.
- Supply specific details of how your solution would work.

Grade 4 Theme 4: Problem Solvers   Challenge Master **CH 4–2**

Activities

Challenge Master CH 4–3

THEME 4/ *Marven of the Great North Woods*

Name _____

1. A Change in Cast

Goal: Change the plot of a story by adding, removing, or changing a main character. Present your new story.

Choose the Story

If a new character is added or a main character is changed, plots can take unexpected turns.

- Choose a favorite story and list the main characters.
- Map out the plot on a story map.

Make one of the following changes:

- Take out a main character.
- Replace a main character with a new character.
- Add a new character.
- Change something important about a main character.

TIPS

- Be sure changes to the plot fit the characters.
- Think about whether a new conflict would result from your character change.

Plot the Effects

Using a new story map, show how your change will affect the plot. Think about how your change affects other characters, the conflict, and the resolution of the conflict.

Share What You Know

Decide how to present your work to the class. You might:

- Use the story maps or act out a key scene to show "before" and "after."
- Retell the story or draw a comic strip with its new ending.

CH 4–3 Challenge Master   Grade 4 Theme 4: Problem Solvers

Copyright © Houghton Mifflin Company. All rights reserved.

Expected Outcome

A good alteration will include

✔ an altered character who is both interesting and believable

✔ developments that are consistent with the characters' natures

✔ a story resolution that works with the altered story elements

1. A Change in Cast

150 MINUTES   INDIVIDUAL   SMALL GROUP

Materials: Graphic Organizer Master 3, drawing paper, poster board, crayons, and markers

DAY 1

Choose the Story

Tell students that if they have chosen to add or alter a character, they might find it helpful to write a character sketch describing the new character. Explain that removing the main character when there is only one is not an option.

DAY 2

Students continue to work on this project.

DAY 3

Plot the Effects

Check with students on the progress of their modifications. Tell students that they may find that they have to struggle to get the plot to come out the way they want it to. If this happens, they should rework their stories and make new character changes until the plot works.

DAY 4

Students continue to work on this project.

DAY 5

Share What You Know

Allow students time to pull together their presentations. Lead a discussion among students and their audience that talks about the challenges involved in altering a story.

2. *Who Stole* The Wizard of Oz?

60 MINUTES   INDIVIDUAL   PAIR

(Challenge Theme Paperback)

Remind students that their altered summary will work best if they make small or subtle changes.

3. Prize-Winning Problem Solvers

60 MINUTES   INDIVIDUAL

(Social Studies)

Materials: reference sources, such as almanacs and encyclopedias, and **Graphic Organizer Master 1**

Emphasize that the point of this activity is to show that one way of solving a large problem is to break it down into smaller parts and work on each one. Refer students to page 24 of the Practice Book for additional support.

Additional Independent Work
Connecting/Comparing Literature

Have students compare the Leveled Reader selection *Samuel de Champlain in Canada* with the anthology selection *Marven of the Great North Woods,* using what they have learned about Problem Solving. Students may discuss or write about their comparisons.

Other Activities

- Challenge Theme Paperback, *Who Stole* The Wizard of Oz?
- Theme 4 Assignment Cards 5, 6, 7
- TE p. 442, Literature Discussion
- TE p. 449, Health
- TE p. 449E, Challenge Word Practice

- TE pp. R6, R11, R19, Challenge
- Education Place: www.eduplace.com More activities related to *Marven of the Great North Woods*
- Accelerated Reader®, *Marven of the Great North Woods*

---

②

Expected Outcome

A good false summary will include

✔ subtle but possible changes

✔ a focus on important events

✔ information on characters, setting, and plot

③

Expected Outcome

A good chart will include

✔ a specific problem the subject worked on

✔ the sequential steps he or she took

✔ the solution that led to the Nobel Peace Prize

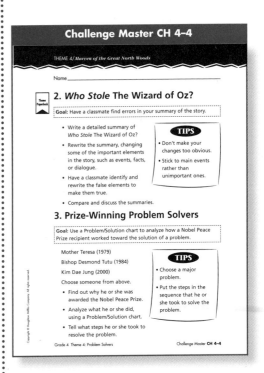

Activities

Challenge Master CH 4–5

THEME 4/*The Last Dragon*

Name _____

1. From Parts to Whole

Goal: Divide the tasks of a project among several group members or small teams and work together to complete the project.

Choose the Project

Dividing responsibility for a project gets it done. First, as a group, choose a project that has several parts or steps. You might:

- Create a reading mural made up of several different panels.
- Create an alphabet or number book for younger students.
- Construct an illustrated time line for a scientific discovery or invention, such as the telephone.

Division of Labor

Divide the tasks among your small teams. Use these guidelines:

- Each task should be about equal in work and easy to understand.
- The teams will need someone to track and organize all the parts.
- Focus on working together.

TIPS

- When choosing or assigning tasks, consider the talents of team members.
- Be sure that all the tasks in the project are assigned or chosen.

Share What You Know

Put the parts together. Then give an oral presentation to the class. Have a spokesperson from each team explain how his or her group worked together to complete the project.

CH 4–5 Challenge Master   Grade 4 Theme 4: Problem Solvers

Copyright © Houghton Mifflin Company. All rights reserved.

---

①

Expected Outcome

A good project will include

✔ good design and accurate text

✔ assignment or division of tasks to group members or small teams

✔ group work that completes the project successfully on time

---

1. From Parts to Whole   150 MINUTES   SMALL GROUP
(Social Studies)

Materials: reference sources, construction paper, poster board, crayons, markers, scissors, and glue

DAY 1

Choose the Project

Emphasize to students that they are to develop a project that can be completed with materials on hand in the time available. Remind them to generate and discuss several ideas before proceeding.

DAY 2

Students continue to work on this project.

DAY 3

Division of Labor

Check with students on their progress in assigning tasks. Emphasize that the activity involves problem solving—how to work in a group to produce an acceptable product. Tell them this kind of problem solving requires

- organization
- cooperation
- self-checking

DAY 4

Students continue to work on this project.

DAY 5

Share What You Know

Have students evaluate their projects by creating a chart that summarizes what they learned from the experience. Have group or team members share positive feedback with everyone for his or her contributions. Have students discuss ways to improve on their process.

2. Beyond the Frame   60 MINUTES   INDIVIDUAL   PAIR
(Art)

Materials: art reproductions and **Graphic Organizer Master 8**

Point out to students that each person brings his or her own experiences to viewing art. Sharing observations about the art creates a better understanding.

3. The Spelling Dragon

60 MINUTES   INDIVIDUAL   PAIR   SMALL GROUP

Materials: poster board, crayons, markers, small colored squares or circles (markers), index or oaktag cards

Students might want to expand the game with other spelling words.

Additional Independent Work
Connecting/Comparing Literature

Have students compare the Leveled Reader selection *I Know, I Know!* with the anthology selection *The Last Dragon,* using what they have learned about Drawing Conclusions. Students may discuss or write about their comparisons.

Other Activities

- Theme 4 Assignment Cards 8, 9, 10
- TE p. 478, Literature Discussion
- TE p. 485, Art
- TE p. 485E, Challenge Word Practice

- TE pp. R13, R21, Challenge
- Education Place: www.eduplace.com More activities related to *The Last Dragon*
- Accelerated Reader®, *The Last Dragon*

2

Expected Outcome

A good conclusion will include

✔ specific details

✔ an evaluation of the artwork

✔ one or more observations about the artwork

3

Expected Outcome

A good game will include

✔ a dragon-shaped game on a poster board

✔ a set of cards with the spelling words for the selection

✔ a demonstrated ability to spell the selected words

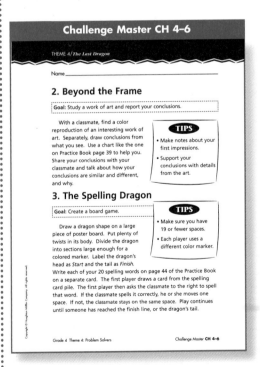

Challenge Master CH 4–6

THEME 4/*The Last Dragon*

Name

2. Beyond the Frame

Goal: Study a work of art and report your conclusions.

With a classmate, find a color reproduction of an interesting work of art. Separately, draw conclusions from what you see. Use a chart like the one on Practice Book page 39 to help you. Share your conclusions with your classmate and talk about how your conclusions are similar and different, and why.

TIPS
- Make notes about your first impressions.
- Support your conclusions with details from the art.

3. The Spelling Dragon

Goal: Create a board game.

Draw a dragon shape on a large piece of poster board. Put plenty of twists in its body. Divide the dragon into sections large enough for a colored marker. Label the dragon's head as *Start* and the tail as *Finish*. Write each of your 20 spelling words on page 44 of the Practice Book on a separate card. The first player draws a card from the spelling card pile. The first player then asks the classmate to the right to spell that word. If the classmate spells it correctly, he or she moves one space. If not, the classmate stays on the same space. Play continues until someone has reached the finish line, or the dragon's tail.

TIPS
- Make sure you have 19 or fewer spaces.
- Each player uses a different color marker.

Grade 4 Theme 4: Problem Solvers   Challenge Master **CH 4–6**

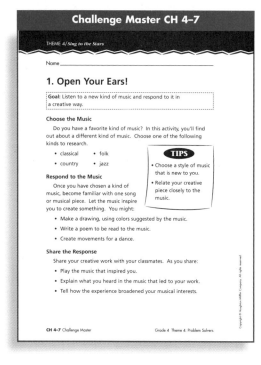

Challenge Master CH 4–7

THEME 4/ *Sing to the Stars*

Name _____

1. Open Your Ears!

Goal: Listen to a new kind of music and respond to it in a creative way.

Choose the Music

Do you have a favorite kind of music? In this activity, you'll find out about a different kind of music. Choose one of the following kinds to research.

- classical
- folk
- country
- jazz

TIPS
- Choose a style of music that is new to you.
- Relate your creative piece closely to the music.

Respond to the Music

Once you have chosen a kind of music, become familiar with one song or musical piece. Let the music inspire you to create something. You might:

- Make a drawing, using colors suggested by the music.
- Write a poem to be read to the music.
- Create movements for a dance.

Share the Response

Share your creative work with your classmates. As you share:

- Play the music that inspired you.
- Explain what you heard in the music that led to your work.
- Tell how the experience broadened your musical interests.

CH 4–7 Challenge Master   Grade 4 Theme 4: Problem Solvers

---

①

Expected Outcome

A good response will include

✔ an analysis of a different kind of music

✔ work related to the specific musical piece

✔ a creative work

---

1. Open Your Ears! <u>150 MINUTES</u>   INDIVIDUAL
(Music) (Art)

Materials: *CDs or tapes of classical, folk, country, and jazz; CD or tape player with earphones; poster board, construction paper, crayons, markers, and paints*

DAY 1

Choose the Music

Advise students to listen to the selection as music, not as a kind of music.

English Language Learners: Students might offer music from their primary cultures as styles for others to choose from.

DAY 2

Students continue to work on this project.

DAY 3

Respond to the Music

Check with students on the progress of their responses. Remind them to respond

- to their own feelings about the music
- in a medium that suits both their interests and the music

DAY 4

Students continue to work on this project.

DAY 5

Share the Response

You may wish to have students follow up their presentations by discussing, as a group, how their attitudes toward different kinds of music may have broadened or changed.

2. Sequels and Structures

<u>60 MINUTES</u>   INDIVIDUAL

Materials: *Graphic Organizer Master 3*

As an additional challenge, have students write and illustrate their sequels. Remind students to include the main characters, the setting, the problem to be solved, key events, and the solution in their maps.

3. Making Music   60 MINUTES   INDIVIDUAL

(Music) (Art)

Materials: *large and medium plastic bottles and containers, large rubber bands, old balloons, water*

Allow students time to practice with their instruments.

Additional Independent Work

Connecting/Comparing Literature

Have students compare the Leveled Reader selection *Shaji in New York* with the anthology selection *Sing to the Stars,* using what they have learned about Story Structure. Students may discuss or write about their comparisons.

Other Activities

- Theme 4 Assignment Cards 11, 12, 13
- TE p. 506, Literature Discussion
- TE p. 511E, Challenge Word Practice

- TE pp. R15, R23, Challenge
- Education Place: www.eduplace.com More activities related to *Sing to the Stars*
- Accelerated Reader®, *Sing to the Stars!*

Expected Outcome

A good sequel will include

✔ an interesting beginning, middle, and end

✔ a problem

✔ a resolution that involves Ephram and Mr. Washington

Expected Outcome

A good instrument presentation will include

✔ correct use of materials

✔ a musical and/or rhythmical sound

✔ a well-practiced presentation

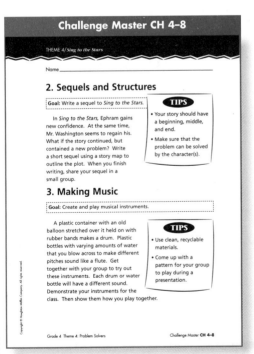

Challenge Master CH 4–8

THEME 4/*Sing to the Stars*

Name _____

2. Sequels and Structures

Goal: Write a sequel to *Sing to the Stars.*

In *Sing to the Stars,* Ephram gains new confidence. At the same time, Mr. Washington seems to regain his. What if the story continued, but contained a new problem? Write a short sequel using a story map to outline the plot. When you finish writing, share your sequel in a small group.

TIPS
- Your story should have a beginning, middle, and end.
- Make sure that the problem can be solved by the character(s).

3. Making Music

Goal: Create and play musical instruments.

A plastic container with an old balloon stretched over it held on with rubber bands makes a drum. Plastic bottles with varying amounts of water that you blow across to make different pitches sound like a flute. Get together with your group to try out these instruments. Each drum or water bottle will have a different sound. Demonstrate your instruments for the class. Then show them how you play together.

TIPS
- Use clean, recyclable materials.
- Come up with a pattern for your group to play during a presentation.

Grade 4 Theme 4: Problem Solvers

Challenge Master **CH 4–8**

Theme 5

Heroes

Selections

1 Happy Birthday, Dr. King!

2 Gloria Estefan

3 Lou Gehrig:
The Luckiest Man

1. A Better Way   150 MINUTES   SMALL GROUP
(Social Studies)

Challenge Master CH 5-1

THEME 5/ *Happy Birthday, Dr. King!*

Name _____

1. A Better Way

Goal: Write and perform a play that shows a peaceful resolution.

Map the Problem

How can you settle disagreements without fighting? Working in a small group, write and perform a play about a peaceful solution to a disagreement. Follow these steps:

- Think of a situation, based on your experiences, that often leads to a disagreement.
- Put the situation into play form. Write out dialogue and actions for each character.
- Assign roles.

TIPS

- Base the disagreement on realistic situations.
- Make the characters and dialogue believable.
- Try to choose a solution that helps both sides.

Choose the Solution

Add a peaceful solution to your play. Use one of these solutions, or another that comes to mind:

- compromising, each side gives up something
- both sides apologizing
- deciding by the flip of a counter
- asking someone outside of the disagreement to decide

Present Your Play

Present your play to the class. At the end of your play, talk with your audience about the disagreement and the peaceful solution. Ask your audience to suggest other peaceful solutions.

CH 5-1 Challenge Master   Grade 4 Theme 5: Heroes

Copyright © Houghton Mifflin Company. All rights reserved.

---

①

Expected Outcome

A good play will include

✔ a realistic situation that involves a disagreement

✔ believable characters and dialogue

✔ a genuinely peaceful resolution of the disagreement

DAY 1

Map the Problem

Remind students to brainstorm and discuss their situations as a group. Tell them to:

- Base the play on a realistic situation for students of their age.
- All the characters should belong to about the same age group.
- Keep the situations general so they appeal to everyone.

English Language Learners: Pair beginners with more advanced students.

DAY 2

Students continue to work on this project.

DAY 3

Choose the Solution

Check with students on their progress. Advise them to work individually to research and sum up ways of peaceful settlement, then discuss them as a group.

DAY 4

Students continue to work on this project.

DAY 5

Present Your Play

Allow students time to rehearse their play. You may want to moderate the discussion about alternative solutions.

2. Civil Rights Quilt   60 MINUTES   SMALL GROUP
(Social Studies) (Art)

Materials: reference sources, including almanacs, crayons, markers, scissors, drawing paper, glue, and backing for the paper quilt

So that students can understand the far-reaching effects of Rosa Parks' act, read aloud the description of the historic meeting between her and Nelson Mandela. You will find the scene on pages 229–231 of Douglas Brinkley's biography *Rosa Parks,* (Penguin Lives, 2000).

3. The Inspiration, Poetry

60 MINUTES   INDIVIDUAL   PAIR

Materials: The Collected Poems of Langston Hughes (Vintage Classics, 1995); other poetry anthologies

Guide students to two Langston Hughes poems, the short "I, Too" and "Freedom's Plow." Your school or public library may have a copy of *Freedom's Children: Young Civil Rights Activists Tell Their Own Stories* by Ellen Levine (Putnam, 1993). African American southerners who were involved in the civil rights struggles of the 1950s and 1960s describe their feelings and experiences.

Additional Independent Work
Connecting/Comparing Literature

Have students compare the Leveled Reader selection *Changing the Rules* with the anthology selection *Happy Birthday, Dr. King!,* using what they have learned about Cause and Effect. Students may discuss or write about their comparisons.

Other Activities

- Theme 5 Assignment Cards 1, 2, 3
- TE p. 548, Literature Discussion
- TE p. 555, Historic Sites
- TE p. 555E, Challenge Word Practice

- TE pp. R9, R15,Challenge
- Education Place: www.eduplace.com
  More activities related to *Happy Birthday, Dr. King!*
- Accelerated Reader®, *Happy Birthday, Dr. King!*

---

❷

Expected Outcome

A good quilt will include

✔ a picture and short biography about each person

✔ an organized design

✔ a statement of each person's deeds and of his or her role in promoting civil rights

❸

Expected Outcome

A good poetry reading will include

✔ a stirring interpretation

✔ an explanation of the poem's affect on its readers

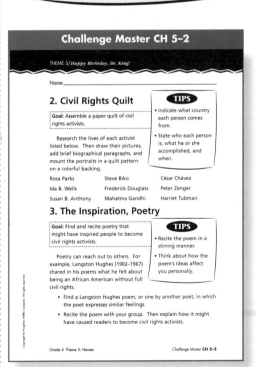

Challenge Master CH 5-2

THEME 5/*Happy Birthday, Dr. King!*

Name _____

2. Civil Rights Quilt

Goal: Assemble a paper quilt of civil rights activists.

Research the lives of each activist listed below. Then draw their pictures, add brief biographical paragraphs, and mount the portraits in a quilt pattern on a colorful backing.

Rosa Parks	Steve Biko	César Chávez
Ida B. Wells	Frederick Douglass	Peter Zenger
Susan B. Anthony	Mahatma Gandhi	Harriet Tubman

TIPS
- Indicate what country each person comes from.
- State who each person is, what he or she accomplished, and when.

3. The Inspiration, Poetry

Goal: Find and recite poetry that might have inspired people to become civil rights activists.

Poetry can reach out to others. For example, Langston Hughes (1902–1967) shared in his poems what he felt about being an African American without full civil rights.

- Find a Langston Hughes poem, or one by another poet, in which the poet expresses similar feelings.
- Recite the poem with your group. Then explain how it might have caused readers to become civil rights activists.

TIPS
- Recite the poem in a stirring manner.
- Think about how the poem's ideas affect you personally.

Grade 4 Theme 5: Heroes   Challenge Master **CH 5-2**

Activities

Challenge Master CH 5–3

THEME 5/ *Gloria Estefan*

Name _____

1. The Benefits of Biography

Goal: Hold a panel discussion on the purposes and benefits of reading biographies.

Go to the Source

Why do people read biographies? For ideas:

• Recall a biography you especially liked.

• Reread or skim it. List the qualities that most appeal to you.

• Highlight the qualities you would look for in other biographies.

Make Your Argument

Prepare your ideas for the panel discussion. Organize your thoughts about biographies into categories. For example, people read biographies

• to learn (about a period of time, career, or field of study)

• to be inspired

• to find a role model

• to satisfy curiosity

TIPS
• Think through your ideas.
• Use examples to back up your opinions.

Discuss Your Thoughts

Hold a panel discussion. Share your ideas on the benefits of reading biographies. Follow these guidelines:

• Choose a moderator to guide the discussion.

• Have the moderator pose questions, such as, "Should students be required to read biographies, and if so, why?"

• Invite questions from the audience after the discussion.

CH 5–3 Challenge Master   Grade 4 Theme 5: Heroes

Copyright © Houghton Mifflin Company. All rights reserved.

1

Expected Outcome

A good panel discussion will include

✔ well-thought-out and organized ideas

✔ specific examples to back up opinions

✔ a lively exchange of ideas

1. The Benefits of Biography

150 MINUTES   SMALL GROUP

(Social Studies)
Materials: biographies

DAY 1

Go to the Source

Tell students to concentrate on their personal reasons for reading biographies, then use those reasons as a basis for thinking about what others might gain from biographies.

English Language Learners: Pair beginners with more experienced learners who can discuss with them any biographies they may have read in their primary language.

DAY 2

Students continue to work on this project.

DAY 3

Make Your Argument

Check with students on the organization of their thoughts.

DAY 4

Students continue to work on this project.

DAY 5

Discuss Your Thoughts

Remind students on the panel to speak slowly and clearly. Students in the audience should raise their hands if they have a question. Remind all students to let each student finish speaking.

2. *The Wreck of the* Ethie 60 MINUTES INDIVIDUAL
(Challenge Theme Paperback)

Materials: The Wreck of the *Ethie and* **Graphic Organizer Master 5**

Remind students that there is no one correct answer because judgments are opinions. However, they should always back up their opinions with specific information.

3. Appealing for Help 60 MINUTES INDIVIDUAL

Materials: reference sources

Remind students that the purpose of a persuasive letter is to convince the recipient to take a specific action. The letter should avoid unrelated information. Tell students this should not be a fan letter.

Additional Independent Work

Connecting/Comparing Literature

Have students compare the Leveled Reader selection *Daniel Inouye: Hero from Hawaii* with the anthology selection *Gloria Estefan,* using what they have learned about Making Judgments. Students may discuss or write about their comparisons.

Other Activities

- Challenge Theme Paperback, *The Wreck of the* Ethie
- Theme 5 Assignment Cards 4, 5, 6
- TE p. 576, Literature Discussion
- TE p. 581E, Challenge Word Practice
- TE pp. R6, R11, R17, Challenge

- Education Place: www.eduplace.com More activities related to *Gloria Estefan*
- Accelerated Reader®, *Gloria Estefan*

Expected Outcome

A good judgment chart will include

✓ clearly stated opinions

✓ reasons that support the judgment

✓ a conclusion that summarizes the judgment

Expected Outcome

A good persuasive letter will include

✓ an appealing cause

✓ strong reasons to support the cause

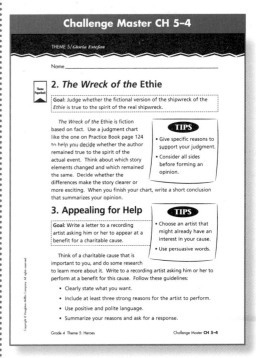

Challenge Master CH 5–4

THEME 5/ *Gloria Estefan*

Name_____

2. *The Wreck of the* Ethie

Goal: Judge whether the fictional version of the shipwreck of the *Ethie* is true to the spirit of the real shipwreck.

The Wreck of the Ethie is fiction based on fact. Use a judgment chart like the one on Practice Book page 124 to help you decide whether the author remained true to the spirit of the actual event. Think about which story elements changed and which remained the same. Decide whether the differences make the story clearer or more exciting. When you finish your chart, write a short conclusion that summarizes your opinion.

TIPS
- Give specific reasons to support your judgment.
- Consider all sides before forming an opinion.

3. Appealing for Help

Goal: Write a letter to a recording artist asking him or her to appear at a benefit for a charitable cause.

TIPS
- Choose an artist that might already have an interest in your cause.
- Use persuasive words.

Think of a charitable cause that is important to you, and do some research to learn more about it. Write to a recording artist asking him or her to perform at a benefit for this cause. Follow these guidelines:
- Clearly state what you want.
- Include at least three strong reasons for the artist to perform.
- Use positive and polite language.
- Summarize your reasons and ask for a response.

Grade 4 Theme 5: Heroes   Challenge Master **CH 5–4**

Activities

Challenge Master CH 5–5

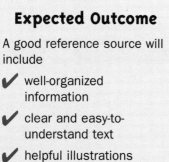

THEME 5/*Lou Gehrig: The Luckiest Man*

Name _____

1. Equipped for Baseball

Goal: Work in small groups to explain and illustrate a reference source on baseball equipment.

Choose the Items

To help a newcomer, make an easy-to-use reference source that explains different pieces of baseball equipment.

• Brainstorm a list of baseball equipment.
• Write the name of each item on an index card.
• Divide the cards among the group.

Research Their Uses

Consult encyclopedias and sports books.

• Make notes on the index cards.
• Name the source that gave you the information.
• On separate sheets of paper, sketch the items and write a one-paragraph explanation for each.

TIPS
• Divide the writing and drawing tasks among your group.
• Choose a publishing method that presents the information clearly and easily.

Publish Your Work

Decide how to present your information. You could create

• a sports dictionary
• a baseball magazine
• sports flash cards

Share your work with the class.

Copyright © Houghton Mifflin Company. All rights reserved.

CH 5–5 Challenge Master   Grade 4 Theme 5: Heroes

---

❶

Expected Outcome

A good reference source will include

✔ well-organized information

✔ clear and easy-to-understand text

✔ helpful illustrations

---

1. Equipped for Baseball

<u>150 MINUTES</u>   SMALL GROUP

(Sports)

Materials: *reference sources, index cards, crayons, and markers*

DAY 1

Choose the Items

Tell students to divide the research evenly among the group members.

English Language Learners: Brainstorm with students different kinds of baseball equipment.

DAY 2

Students continue to work on this project.

DAY 3

Research Their Uses

Check with students on the progress of their information gathering. Tell students to think of what is the most useful information to have about any piece of equipment. They should use that information as the main idea of their explanatory paragraph. They may have to draw an object from different perspectives to clarify its shape.

DAY 4

Students continue to work on this project.

DAY 5

Publish Your Work

Remind students that their goal is to make their presentation easy to understand. Students should test any parts they are not sure of on classmates who are new to baseball.

2. Heroes 60 MINUTES INDIVIDUAL

Remind students that they can choose someone famous or someone they know personally. Ask volunteers to share their essays with the class. For additional reading, have students read *Marie Curie* from the Houghton Mifflin Classroom Bookshelf.

3. The Fact or Opinion Game

60 MINUTES INDIVIDUAL

Materials: *poster board, index cards, markers, and reference sources*

Students might use statements about baseball from their text, Practice Book, or other source.

Additional Independent Work

Connecting/Comparing Literature

Have students compare the Leveled Reader selection *Roberto Clemente: Baseball Superstar* with the anthology selection *Lou Gehrig: The Luckiest Man*, using what they have learned about Fact and Opinion. Students may discuss or write about their comparisons.

Other Activities

- Theme 5 Assignment Cards 7, 8, 9, 10
- TE p. 602, Literature Discussion
- TE p. 607E, Challenge Word Practice

- TE pp. R13, R19, R21, Challenge
- Education Place: www.eduplace.com More activities related to *Lou Gehrig: The Luckiest Man*
- Accelerated Reader®, *Lou Gehrig: The Luckiest Man*

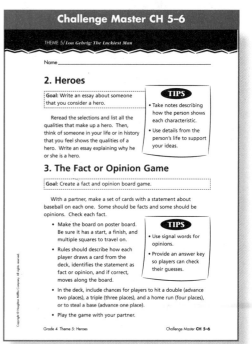

2

Expected Outcome

A good essay will include

✔ someone who has heroic qualities

✔ details to support the choice

✔ an understanding of the theme

3

Expected Outcome

A good game will include

✔ factual statements

✔ opinion statements

✔ clear playing directions

Challenge Master CH 5–6

THEME 5/ *Lou Gehrig: The Luckiest Man*

Name _____

2. Heroes

Goal: Write an essay about someone that you consider a hero.

Reread the selections and list all the qualities that make up a hero. Then, think of someone in your life or in history that you feel shows the qualities of a hero. Write an essay explaining why he or she is a hero.

TIPS
- Take notes describing how the person shows each characteristic.
- Use details from the person's life to support your ideas.

3. The Fact or Opinion Game

Goal: Create a fact and opinion board game.

With a partner, make a set of cards with a statement about baseball on each one. Some should be facts and some should be opinions. Check each fact.

- Make the board on poster board. Be sure it has a start, a finish, and multiple squares to travel on.
- Rules should describe how each player draws a card from the deck, identifies the statement as fact or opinion, and if correct, moves along the board.
- In the deck, include chances for players to hit a double (advance two places), a triple (three places), and a home run (four places), or to steal a base (advance one place).
- Play the game with your partner.

TIPS
- Use signal words for opinions.
- Provide an answer key so players can check their guesses.

Grade 4 Theme 5: Heroes   Challenge Master **CH 5–6**

Copyright © Houghton Mifflin Company. All rights reserved.

Theme 6

Nature: Friend and Foe

Selections

1 Salmon Summer

2 Wildfires

3 Skylark

1. Kodiak Island Experts

<u>150 MINUTES</u>   SMALL GROUP

(Social Studies)

Materials: reference materials, index cards, and a jar or small box

DAY 1

Choose Your Questions

Remind students to brainstorm enough questions so that each member of the group (except the moderator) has two questions. Tell them to choose questions that interest them.

English Language Learners: Explain the term *expert* to students and what it means to be an expert.

DAY 2

Students continue to work on this project.

DAY 3

Become an Expert

Check with students on their progress. Be sure they gather enough information to answer the questions thoroughly. Remind them that their notes should be words and phrases to help them remember information.

DAY 4

Students continue to work on this project.

DAY 5

Inform the Class

Invite other classes to be part of the question and answer audience.

Challenge Master CH 6–1

THEME 6/*Salmon Summer*

Name _____

1. Kodiak Island Experts

Goal: Take part in a question and answer session about Kodiak Island.

TIPS
• Use your notes to guide you. Do not read from your notes.
• You should have most of the information committed to memory.
• Be sure to answer your questions completely.

Choose Your Questions

You and a group of classmates are going to become experts on Kodiak Island. As a group, brainstorm a list of questions about Kodiak Island. Reread *Salmon Summer* and read other reference sources to help you. Choose one member of your group as moderator. He or she will ask the questions. Each group member should choose two questions to research.

Become an Expert

• When you have chosen your two questions, research Kodiak Island and take notes on each question.
• Once you have completed your research, make notes on index cards that you will use to answer your questions.
• The moderator should write out each question on a slip of paper and put all the questions into a jar or box.

Inform the Class

Have a question and answer session for your class.
• The moderator will ask volunteers to draw a question from the jar or box.
• The moderator reads the question aloud, and the expert whose question is read stands and answers the question.

CH 6–1 Challenge Master   Grade 4 Theme 6: Nature: Friend or Foe

Copyright © Houghton Mifflin Company. All rights reserved.

---

①

Expected Outcome

A good question and answer session will include

✔ good questions about Kodiak Island

✔ answers that are well researched and complete

✔ a well-moderated discussion

---

2. Hidden Ocean Treasure

60 MINUTES   INDIVIDUAL   PAIR

Materials: ocean objects, such as sea shells or plastic ocean fish

Remind students to use order and direction words in their writing. If time allows, have students repeat the activity more than twice.

3. Catch and Release: A Debate

30 MINUTES   INDIVIDUAL

Materials: reference sources

Review or introduce classroom rules for conducting a debate. You might want to moderate the debate. Students can find one side of the argument on-line at the home page of the Alaska Department of Fish and Game at
http://www.state.ak.us/adfg/sportf/geninfo/selhar/c&r.htm

Additional Independent Work
Connecting/Comparing Literature

Have students compare the Leveled Reader selection *Help with the Herd* with the anthology selection *Salmon Summer,* using what they have learned about Following Directions. Students may discuss or write about their comparisons.

Other Activities

- Theme 6 Assignment Cards 1, 2, 3
- TE p. 646, Literature Discussion
- TE p. 653, Science
- TE p. 653E, Challenge Word Practice

- TE pp. R9, R15, Challenge
- Education Place: www.eduplace.com More activities related to *Salmon Summer*
- Accelerated Reader®, *Salmon Summer*

Expected Outcome

A good treasure hunt will include

✔ a hidden ocean object

✔ a clear set of directions using order and direction words

✔ discovery of the object

Expected Outcome

A good debate will include

✔ well-prepared and well-developed arguments

✔ persuasive speaking

✔ courteous exchanges between debaters

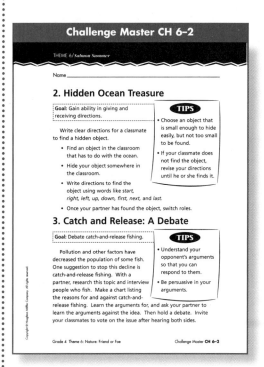

Challenge Master CH 6-2

THEME 6/*Salmon Summer*

Name _____

2. Hidden Ocean Treasure

Goal: Gain ability in giving and receiving directions.

Write clear directions for a classmate to find a hidden object.

- Find an object in the classroom that has to do with the ocean.
- Hide your object somewhere in the classroom.
- Write directions to find the object using words like *start, right, left, up, down, first, next,* and *last.*
- Once your partner has found the object, switch roles.

TIPS
- Choose an object that is small enough to hide easily, but not too small to be found.
- If your classmate does not find the object, revise your directions until he or she finds it.

3. Catch and Release: A Debate

Goal: Debate catch-and-release fishing.

Pollution and other factors have decreased the population of some fish. One suggestion to stop this decline is catch-release fishing. With a partner, research this topic and interview people who fish. Make a chart listing the reasons for and against catch-and-release fishing. Learn the arguments for, and ask your partner to learn the arguments against the idea. Then hold a debate. Invite your classmates to vote on the issue after hearing both sides.

TIPS
- Understand your opponent's arguments so that you can respond to them.
- Be persuasive in your arguments.

Grade 4 Theme 6: Nature: Friend or Foe

Challenge Master **CH 6-2**

Activities

Challenge Master CH 6–3

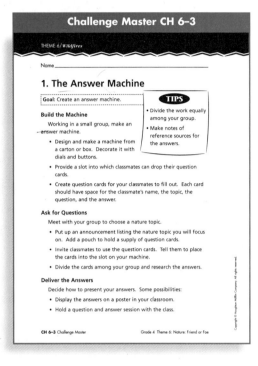

THEME 6/*Wildfires*

Name _____

1. The Answer Machine

Goal: Create an answer machine.

Build the Machine
Working in a small group, make an answer machine.

• Design and make a machine from a carton or box. Decorate it with dials and buttons.

• Provide a slot into which classmates can drop their question cards.

• Create question cards for your classmates to fill out. Each card should have space for the classmate's name, the topic, the question, and the answer.

Ask for Questions
Meet with your group to choose a nature topic.

• Put up an announcement listing the nature topic you will focus on. Add a pouch to hold a supply of question cards.

• Invite classmates to use the question cards. Tell them to place the cards into the slot on your machine.

• Divide the cards among your group and research the answers.

Deliver the Answers
Decide how to present your answers. Some possibilities:

• Display the answers on a poster in your classroom.

• Hold a question and answer session with the class.

TIPS
• Divide the work equally among your group.
• Make notes of reference sources for the answers.

Copyright © Houghton Mifflin Company. All rights reserved.

CH 6–3 Challenge Master   Grade 4 Theme 6: Nature: Friend or Foe

❶ Expected Outcome

A good answer machine will include

✔ well-researched answers

✔ a record of the reference source used

✔ a direct response to each question

1. The Answer Machine   150 MINUTES   SMALL GROUP

(Science)

Materials: *reference sources, cartons or boxes, oaktag cards, drawing paper, crayons, markers, paint, construction paper, poster board, and glue*

DAY 1

Build the Machine

To encourage cooperation, suggest the following:

• Have group members assign a student to sketch the group's idea for the answer machine.

• When the group has approved the design, have a pair of students carry out the design.

English Language Learners: Pair beginners with more advanced students.

DAY 2

Students continue to work on this project.

DAY 3

Ask for Questions

Check with students on the progress of their answer machine. Tell them that they should

• narrow their topic so that they can use available reference sources

• make the purpose of the answer box clear to the class

• persuade students to submit questions

DAY 4

Students continue to work on this project.

DAY 5

Deliver the Answers

If students choose an oral presentation format, there may not be sufficient time to answer all questions. Remind them that they should think of an alternate way of responding to leftover questions.

2. The Good Side of Volcanoes

60 MINUTES   INDIVIDUAL   PAIR

*Materials: reference sources and **Graphic Organizer Master 4***

Have students check a dictionary to make sure they understand the word *benefits*. Students should understand that the negative effects of an eruption can be very serious.

3. *Water Hole: Life in a Rescued Tropical Forest*   60 MINUTES   INDIVIDUAL

(Challenge Theme Paperback)

(Science) (Art)

Materials: drawing paper, crayons, markers, and paints

Tell students that by translating their impressions into an art form, they are trying to capture the *effect* of the experience on them.

Additional Independent Work

Connecting/Comparing Literature

Have students compare the Leveled Reader selection *Beating the Heat, Desert Style* with the anthology selection *Wildfires,* using what they have learned about Topic, Main Idea, and Details. Students may discuss or write about their comparisons.

Other Activities

- Challenge Theme Paperback, *Water Hole: Life in a Rescued Tropical Forest*
- Theme 6 Assignment Cards 4, 5, 6
- TE p. 678, National Parks
- TE p. 680, Literature Discussion
- TE p. 685E, Challenge Word Practice

- TE pp. R6, R11, R17, Challenge
- Education Place: www.eduplace.com More activities related to *Wildfires*
- Accelerated Reader®, *Wildfires*

2

Expected Outcome

A good essay will include

✔ an understanding of the benefits of volcanoes

✔ a topic, main idea, and supporting details

✔ correct spelling and grammar

3

Expected Outcome

A good expression will include

✔ observations from the point of view of the observer

✔ impressions of the tempo or rhythm of the site

✔ evidence of individuality and originality

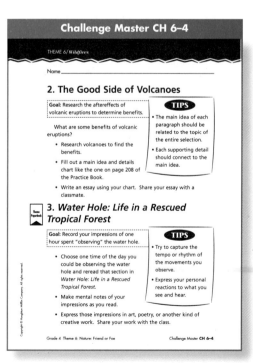

Activities

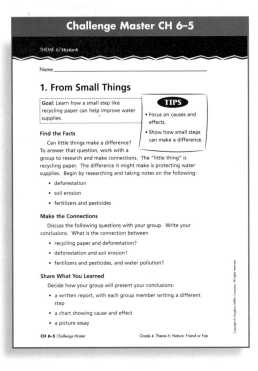

Challenge Master CH 6–5

THEME 6/*Skylark*

Name _____

1. From Small Things

Goal: Learn how a small step like recycling paper can help improve water supplies.

TIPS
- Focus on causes and effects.
- Show how small steps can make a difference.

Find the Facts

Can little things make a difference? To answer that question, work with a group to research and make connections. The "little thing" is recycling paper. The difference it might make is protecting water supplies. Begin by researching and taking notes on the following:

- deforestation
- soil erosion
- fertilizers and pesticides

Make the Connections

Discuss the following questions with your group. Write your conclusions. What is the connection between

- recycling paper and deforestation?
- deforestation and soil erosion?
- fertilizers and pesticides, and water pollution?

Share What You Learned

Decide how your group will present your conclusions:

- a written report, with each group member writing a different step
- a chart showing cause and effect
- a picture essay

CH 6–5 Challenge Master   Grade 4 Theme 6: Nature: Friend or Foe

1

Expected Outcome

A good presentation will include

✔ details about each topic

✔ a focus on cause and effect relationships

✔ the connections between recycling paper and conserving water supplies

1. From Small Things 150 MINUTES   SMALL GROUP
(Social Studies) (Science)

Materials: reference sources, poster board, crayons, markers, glue, and scissors

DAY 1

Find the Facts

Tell students to discover connections from information they gather about each topic. Students should divide the research equally among group members. You may wish to make available the following books published by Earth Works Group: *50 Simple Things Kids Can Do to Save the Earth* and *50 Simple Things Kids Can Do to Recycle.*

English Language Learners: Pair beginners with more advanced students.

DAY 2

Students continue to work on this project.

DAY 3

Make the Connections

Check with students on the progress of their information gathering. Tell them to summarize their research and share it with other members of the group. Advise them to take notes on the group discussion.

DAY 4

Students continue to work on this project.

DAY 5

Share What You Learned

Each student in the group should contribute to the final presentation.

2. Caleb's Story *60 MINUTES* INDIVIDUAL

Materials: anthology

Have students refer to story events and details that will make their story seem authentic. Students should make Caleb's character consistent with the author's view.

3. Nature: Friend or Foe? *60 MINUTES* INDIVIDUAL

Ask volunteers to share their speeches with the class.

Additional Independent Work
Connecting/Comparing Literature

Have students compare the Leveled Reader selection *Jewel of the Desert* with the anthology selection *Skylark,* using what they have learned about Making Inferences. Students may discuss or write about their comparisons.

Other Activities

- Theme 6 Assignment Cards 7, 8, 9, 10
- TE p. 702, Literature Discussion
- TE p. 707E, Challenge Word Practice

- TE pp. R13, R19, Challenge
- Education Place: www.eduplace.com More activities related to *Skylark*
- Accelerated Reader®, *Skylark*

Expected Outcome

A good telling will include

✔ events retold from Caleb's point of view

✔ important details relating specifically to Caleb

✔ a believable portrayal of Caleb's feelings

Expected Outcome

A good speech will include

✔ facts or events in a clear order

✔ interesting details about the topic

✔ a closing sentence

✔ persuasive and interesting language

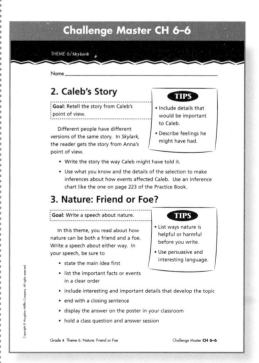

Blackline Masters for Grade 4

Activity Masters

Graphic Organizer Masters

Name_____

1. Tell Me Your Journey

Goal: Interview someone you know about a journey he or she has taken. Retell or present the journey to classmates.

Think About a Journey

Think about someone you know who has taken a journey or trip. It could be a parent, relative, friend, teacher, or someone in your community.

- Write down what you already know about the person's journey.
- Write down what you want to know about the journey.

Questions for the Interview

Read the information you wrote. Do the facts fit together well or is something missing?

- When, where, and why did you go on the journey?
- What did you see during the journey?
- Why was the journey important to you?

TIPS

- Think about your format before your interview. For a time line, ask about dates.
- Ask about details of the journey and how the person you are interviewing felt. Use direct quotations.

Sharing the Story

Choose a format for retelling the journey. For example:

- Write and illustrate a booklet; write a newspaper article or a long poem.
- Create a map or time line, with captions.
- Make a display center with objects from the journey.

Copyright © Houghton Mifflin Company. All rights reserved.

Name_____

2. A New Point of View

Goal: Retell a story scene from a new point of view.

Change the narration in *Akiak.* Choose a scene from the story and write it from the point of view of one of the other characters. For example:

- Mick or another musher
- Akiak or another dog
- the man who let Akiak out the back door

TIPS

- Think about details that bring a story to life. What would the character see, hear, and remember?
- Think about the character's feelings in that scene. How would those feelings affect the way he or she tells the story?

3. Follow That Story!

Goal: Read two news stories and compare them in writing.

Find two news stories on the same topic. Write a short paper that compares how reporters describe the events and how they use quotations in each. Tell which news story you like best and explain why.

TIPS

- Look for facts about the topic used in both stories to help you make comparisons.
- Make a list of people quoted in each story and what they said.
- Jot down details that support your choice for best story.

Copyright © Houghton Mifflin Company. All rights reserved.

Name_____

1. Story Circle

Goal: Learn a story from another country or culture and share it with the class.

Find a Common Theme

Find examples of stories from different cultures that share a theme or subject, such as bravery, overcoming problems, or wisdom.

- In a small group, discuss how the stories are alike and different.

- Each member of the group will then choose a story to share.

- Read and reread the story until you know it very well.

- List ways to present your story, such as reading it aloud, presenting it as a play, or using puppets.

Plan the Retelling

Meet with your story circle.

- Based on how much class time your story circle will have, decide how many minutes each member will have to share his or her story.

- Discuss the presentations the group is planning and decide on their order.

Share What You Know

Invite your classmates to hear your stories.

- Create a program naming the story presenters and their stories.

- Form a circle and tell your stories in order.

TIPS

- If your original story is long, choose an important part to read word for word. Summarize the rest.

- Rehearse your presentation in front of a mirror and/or with someone who can give you helpful comments.

- Have fun telling the story.

Copyright © Houghton Mifflin Company. All rights reserved.

Name_____

2. Personal Poetry

Goal: Create poetry from Grandfather's point of view.

Write a poem from Grandfather's point of view that reveals his feelings about his two homes. Find a line from the story that describes how Grandfather felt. Change it to read the way Grandfather might have written it. Add other lines to create a poem that expresses Grandfather's feelings. Copy your final draft onto drawing paper and illustrate it.

TIPS

- Refer to things the author says Grandfather did, felt, and said.

- Use words that show Grandfather's thoughts and feelings.

Theme Paperback

3. *Over the Top of the World*

Goal: Make a list of important information a traveler to the Arctic should know about the region.

Select ten points of information from *Over the Top of the World* that you think are necessary for an explorer's safety. Use resources to define any terms that might be unfamiliar, such as *windchill* and *pressure ridges.* Arrange the information in a numbered list, in order of importance.

TIPS

- For each point, make clear why the information is important.

- Explain how explorers might use the information to stay safe.

Copyright © Houghton Mifflin Company. All rights reserved.

Name_____

1. Extra! Extra!

Goal: Recreate the front page of a local paper as it might have appeared on April 16, 1912, the day after the sinking of the *Titanic.*

Find the Facts

On April 16, 1912, newspapers around the world were full of the news of the sinking of the "unsinkable" *Titanic.*

- Find a current local or national newspaper to use as a model for your front page.

- Look for sources about the sinking, and make notes of the important details.

- Act as if you were the editor. Decide on a name for your newspaper, how many stories you would include, and how many photographs or illustrations would be on the front page.

Writing the Stories

Plan your front page. Each story should have an attention-grabbing headline and at least two supporting paragraphs. Then write one of the stories. Think about the focus of this story and how many details should be included.

TIPS

- Think about your audience; your story should keep your readers' attention.

- Write your story in short, informative sentences to deliver important information quickly.

Share What You Know

- Paste your story, illustrations, and photographs, on a large sheet of paper that will be your front page.

- Display your front page on the bulletin board along with other classmates' front pages.

Copyright © Houghton Mifflin Company. All rights reserved.

Name_____

2. To Preserve or Not to Preserve?

Goal: Write a persuasive essay about whether the *Titanic* should be left undisturbed as a monument or not.

- Support your opinion with strong reasons that appeal to your audience.

- Support your reasons with facts and examples.

- Answer any objections you think your audience might have.

TIPS

- Draft your essay with a strong introduction.

- Use details to explain each reason.

- Order your reasons from least to most important.

- Use positive, confident language.

- End by summing up your reasons and repeating your opinion.

3. Diorama

Goal: Create a diorama of what Robert Ballard and his crew found two and one-half miles down on the bottom of the Atlantic Ocean.

Reread *Finding the* Titanic and make notes about what Robert Ballard found. Think about

- what materials you might work with

- whether to use models, pictures, or realistic materials

- how large to make your diorama

- what kind of explanatory material, if any, to include

TIPS

- Use graph paper to plan your diorama.

- Refer to reference sources for photographs and background data.

Copyright © Houghton Mifflin Company. All rights reserved.

Name_____

1. A Sense-ible Source Book

Goal: Create a source book of the senses.

Brainstorm Topics

First, freely list sense words that come to mind. Include

- images and textures

- words, synonyms, definitions

- examples from magazines, books, television, and other sources

Jot down any other words that come to mind. Then organize your words into categories representing the five senses.

Create the Pages

Using your categorized word lists, make a table of contents for your book.

- Write the sense category, for example, *Sight,* and any words you brainstormed for that category.

- Create a book page for each sense word.

- Include a picture to represent each word.

TIPS

- Be sure that your words are categorized under the right sense.

- Include many descriptive words and images.

Put Your Book Together

Assemble your pages in a book or loose-leaf binder.

- Place your table of contents in the front. Arrange your pages in the order of the table of contents.

- Create an interesting cover that relates to the subject.

Copyright © Houghton Mifflin Company. All rights reserved.

Name_____

2. The First Time I Ever . . .

Goal: Write an essay about the first time you ever did something, using important details to make the description interesting and believable.

Think about the first time you ever did something, such as ride a bike, go to school, or play a sport. Include the following in your writing:

- a description of the situation leading up to the event, during it, and afterward
- the physical and emotional feelings that you experienced
- how the experience helped with later challenges

TIPS

- To get started, list important details.
- Use details and words that capture both your actions and feelings.

3. Seeing Out Loud

Goal: Describe your favorite place so that a classmate can draw a picture of it.

Think about your favorite place. Describe it to a classmate with descriptive words.

- Give the drawer some idea of how much space he or she will need.
- Mention which things are close, which are farther away.
- Compare colors and textures to familiar objects and sights. Finally, talk about the drawing.

TIPS

- Take a moment to get a good picture in your mind of your place.
- Describe only the most important elements of your place.
- Do not look at the drawing until it is completely done.

Copyright © Houghton Mifflin Company. All rights reserved.

Name_____

1. The Library, Live!

> **Goal:** Create interest in a favorite library book by giving a dramatic presentation based on it.

Choose Your Inspiration

When you finish a book you really enjoy, do you tell others about it? Do you wish there were more of it?

- Jot down the names of three library books you have enjoyed, and list things that appealed to you.

- Choose one book to present to your classmates.

Choose Your Scene

Look through the book to

- find passages that show the qualities you like most

- choose a passage that is simple enough to act out

- think how to adapt the passage

You may decide on a monologue, a retelling from one point of view.

TIPS

- Choose a passage that is exciting and will catch your audience's attention.

- Practice in front of a mirror and with a helpful friend.

Show What You Know

Think about how you can present your passage so that it appeals to your audience. Choose one of these ideas or an idea of your own.

- Make stick puppets of a major character or characters to hold up as you act out part of the story.

- Dress up as one character in a simple costume.

Copyright © Houghton Mifflin Company. All rights reserved.

Name_____

2. Meet the Librarian

Goal: Interview your school librarian and report to your class.

Do you know your librarian?

- Set up a time to meet with the school librarian.

- Prepare interview questions ahead of time, such as *Why did you become a librarian?*

- Summarize the information in a newspaper profile to share with the class.

TIPS

- Take good notes or tape record your interview. Ask the librarian to repeat answers if needed.

- In your article, use summaries and direct quotations.

3. From Seedling to Harvest

Goal: Show the sequence of events in the life cycle of a crop—from planting to harvest—and tell its story.

Choose a major crop of Texas or Iowa. Research that crop to find

- how it is planted

- how long it takes to grow

- how it is picked or processed

Present the information as if you were telling a story. Use time words to signal events, such as *in the spring.* To help others understand the life cycle, draw a diagram to go with your story.

TIPS

- Use reference sources.

- Include special details that apply to Iowa or Texas, such as climate, soil, or rainfall.

- Describe what people and machinery do.

Copyright © Houghton Mifflin Company. All rights reserved.

Name_____

1. Road Games

Goal: Publish a book of family games to play on a trip.

Collecting

There are many games that people have invented over the years to make traveling more fun. You can collect your favorites into a book.

- Ask family members and friends for suggestions of games that help pass the time on a long trip.

- Add games or puzzles that you've enjoyed.

- Make notes about each game and how to play it.

Sorting Out

List the kinds of games you want in your book such as games that

- are for all ages

- aren't too noisy

- don't need any special equipment

- might be for only one player

Choose at least ten games that match your list.

Show What You Know

Turn your list into a book. You may want to use a computer to type the pages and make the pictures. Decide how to publish your information.

TIPS

- Start out with more than ten ideas so you have many to choose from. Remember to title each game.

- Write clear directions and find or draw helpful illustrations.

- Group the same kind of games together.

Copyright © Houghton Mifflin Company. All rights reserved.

Name_____

Theme Paperback

2. *In Search of the Grand Canyon*

Goal: Write a report that John Wesley Powell might have written about his journey in *In Search of the Grand Canyon.*

The book *In Search of the Grand Canyon* tells of a thrilling and sometimes dangerous trip. Choose two moments when Powell and his companions saw unfamiliar things and gave them new names. Write a report about those moments.

- Explain where Powell and his companions were and show it on a map of the Grand Canyon.

- Describe, in your own words, what happened.

- Tell what the new names were and why the men chose them.

TIPS

- Present the facts in order.

- Include descriptive words and phrases.

3. A Quality Character

Goal: Write a character sketch of a person whom you admire.

- Choose a person. If necessary, research that person's life.

- Write a short character sketch of that person.

Make an inference chart that shows

- the events or facts you describe in your sketch

TIPS

- Get your information from a dependable source.

- Base your inferences on facts, not on opinions.

- references to similar events or facts from your life

- the inferences you made based on the person's qualities

Copyright © Houghton Mifflin Company. All rights reserved.

Name _____

1. Story Hat

Goal: Become a storyteller and make a hat that gives story choices.

Find the Stories

Imagine that you are a traveling storyteller with a hat that shows the stories you can tell. The stories have the same theme—a person leaves home and finds or does something special. You will need to

- look for stories from different cultures

- find at least three stories based on this theme

- learn the stories by heart

TIPS

- Practice until you can tell each story in about ten minutes or less.

- Follow the guidelines for a good oral presentation: Speak clearly, loudly, slowly, and look at the audience.

Make the Hat

When you have chosen your stories and know them well enough to retell them, make the hat that names the stories.

- Find any kind of hat, for example, a baseball cap or a rain hat.

- Write the titles of the stories on self-stick notes and attach them to the hat.

- Add story-related decorations to your hat.

Share What You Know

Drop your hat and ask a classmate to pick out a story for everyone to hear. Or, visit a reading circle or another class.

Copyright © Houghton Mifflin Company. All rights reserved.

Name_____

2. What's the Reason?

Goal: Make generalizations about why people wear hats.

At times in our country's history more people wore hats. Still, some people *do* wear hats. Why?

- Brainstorm a list of people at work or at play who wear hats.

- Identify the reason that person wears a hat.

- Sort your list into groups. Use your groups to write three generalizations about why people wear hats today.

TIPS

- Use a reference source, if necessary, to fill out your list.

- Make a chart that shows the sorting on which you based your generalization.

3. Song of the West

Goal: Using a traditional tune, write your own lyrics to a song about workers.

Boss of the Plains mentions different workers who sang songs while they worked.

- Learn a song in the anthology or find another traditional song.

- Write a work song for a worker in the selection.

- Write three stanzas and a chorus to the tune of the song you chose.

TIPS

- Look for a song that has a rhythm that suggests the kind of work being done.

- Keep the chorus simple so that your audience can join in.

Copyright © Houghton Mifflin Company. All rights reserved.

Name_____

1. The Start of a New Day

Goal: Suggest a new holiday the democratic way.

Set Up the Choices

What if you could create a new holiday? Use the following steps:

- Form a holiday committee.

- As a group select a moderator to run the meeting, a secretary to take notes, and a recorder to count votes.

- Each committee member will list ideas about what the holiday will honor, its name, and when it will be celebrated.

Vote on the Holiday

Meet again to narrow the choices and discuss favorite ideas. Decide on three of the suggested holidays to put on a ballot. The ballot should have a yes/no format. Distribute the ballots to committee members and hold a vote. The suggestion with the most votes may become the new holiday.

Share What You Know

Create a poster that announces the new holiday. It should

- name the new holiday

- describe its purpose

- declare how it ought to be celebrated

Present your new holiday to the class.

TIPS

- Have the moderator set time limits so that every committee member can take part.

- Write a draft version of the decision so that committee members can review it before presenting it to the class.

Copyright © Houghton Mifflin Company. All rights reserved.

Name_____

2. New Americans' Contributions

Goal: Write a report on the contributions of someone who immigrated to the United States.

Find a famous person who immigrated to the United States. Write a report about him or her. Include

- where the person started from

- when he or she immigrated

- what major contributions this person has made

- why you think this person is important

TIPS

- Think about people who are influential in different areas of life, such as art, music, literature, sports, government, and film.

- Explain why you think this person should be recognized.

3. Sorting States

Goal: Sort the states of the United States into different categories.

How many ways can you categorize the states? Create webs that show the different categories. Use a map to help you. The same state can be used more than once. Share your webs with a classmate and talk about the different categories you chose and why.

TIPS

- List ways to categorize the states, such as geographically, alphabetically, and by size. Use reference sources as needed.

- Use a neat, easy-to-read format.

Copyright © Houghton Mifflin Company. All rights reserved.

Name _____

1. Showing Change Over Time

Goal: Show a change in nature as it occurs over time.

Find the Facts

When leaves change color in the fall, it happens over a period of time. Find an example in nature of this kind of change. Some suggestions:

- the development of a bird from egg to flight

- a plant from seed to flower or to fruit

- a tadpole changing into a frog

Take detailed notes on your research. Write down your reference sources. Check your completed work against them.

Organize and Present the Facts

Think what you might show visually. Decide what you will explain in text.

Choose one of these ideas or an idea of your own:

- a filmstrip (on a roll of paper)

- a series of strips explaining the stages of development

- an illustrated, step-by-step diagram or flowchart

Share What You Know

Give an oral presentation to the class. Provide handouts or models. Have a question-and-answer session.

TIPS

- Label important details of visual aids.

- Write text that helps the class connect the steps.

- Present your information logically.

Copyright © Houghton Mifflin Company. All rights reserved.

Name _____

2. Synonym Dominoes

Goal: Create a synonym matching game based on dominoes.

You can make a game of matching synonyms.

- To begin, collect about 20 pairs of synonyms. Add four words for which you do not have a synonym.

TIPS

- Choose words that you know.
- If necessary, review the rules for dominoes.

- Make domino cards out of index cards. Draw a line down the center of the card and write one word on each side of the line. The two words should not be synonyms.

- Divide the cards equally between you and another classmate.

- Play the game by matching all the synonyms end to end.

3. Drawing Word Pictures

Goal: Make a word picture of a living tree.

TIPS

- Write each detail in the part of the tree it describes.
- Think about the shape of your tree as you place details.

First, research a type of tree and make notes of details, such as leaves, flowers, and fruits, depending on the season; height and trunk size; the shape of the whole tree; and the bark texture and color.

Then create your word picture by writing the details in the shape of your tree.

Copyright © Houghton Mifflin Company. All rights reserved.

Name _____

1. What Really Happened?

> **Goal:** Retell the story *Cendrillon* from different perspectives.

Revisit the Story

- Interview the other main characters in *Cendrillon* to get their versions of events.

- Make one list of questions to ask the characters.

- Each version of the story should have the same events, but will be different depending on each character's point of view.

TIPS

- Reread the story.

- Make a list of the main characters to be sure to interview them all.

- Choose a presentation that will include all the elements of your story.

Compare the Versions

Collect all the versions and put them together to retell the story.

- Make notes for the new version from each interview.

- List all the events in the story.

- Match each event with the character you've picked to tell about it.

- Include something from the point of view of everyone you interview.

- Include the same plot elements that occur in *Cendrillon.*

Share What You Know

Decide how to retell and present your story to the class. You might:

- Present your new story orally.

- Act out your retelling by role-playing the different characters.

- Write and illustrate your version.

Copyright © Houghton Mifflin Company. All rights reserved.

Name_____

Theme Paperback

2. *The Real Thief*

Goal: Write a character sketch of Gawain.

How does Gawain change in the course of the story? Write a two-part character sketch. First, show Gawain before he is accused of theft. Then show how his experience changed him. Share your sketch with a classmate.

TIPS

• Begin by listing Gawain's character traits.

• List an event, or events, that show Gawain using each trait.

3. Island Life

Goal: Compare and contrast life on two islands.

In some ways, living on any island in the West Indies can be similar. But island life can also be very different.

• Research life on Martinique and another island in the West Indies.

• Look for similar or different facts about climate, economy, population, and government.

• Use a three-column format. List what you are comparing and contrasting in the first column. In the other two columns write related facts about the two islands you are researching.

TIPS

• Use an almanac, atlas, and encyclopedia to help you.

• Remember to find *similarities* and *differences* in your research.

Copyright © Houghton Mifflin Company. All rights reserved.

Name _____

1. Telling Tall Tales

Goal: Write and tell a tall tale based on real events.

Tale Hunt

Most tall tales are based on real events, but are called "tall" because the author exaggerates or stretches the details. Read some tall tales to understand why they're called "tall."

TIPS

- Choose a believable event that can be stretched.
- Add many adjectives and verbs.

- List events in your own life that you could turn into a tall tale.

- Choose one event and write down the real things that happened.

- Think about how you could stretch these things to make them amazing.

Write the Tale

Write your tall tale.

- List adjectives and verbs that would make your story taller.

- Think about amazing abilities that you can give yourself and other characters in the tale.

- Draw pictures to go with your tale.

Share What You Know

Tell your tall tale to the class. You might:

- Read your story and show your pictures.

- Use puppets to act out the story or play the different parts yourself.

Copyright © Houghton Mifflin Company. All rights reserved.

Name _____

2. Fact or Fantasy?

Goal: Reject or accept weather sayings after researching them.

Listed below are sayings about the weather. Test them by researching the weather facts that the sayings are based on. Write down what you learn and record your sources.

TIPS

- Find facts to support or disprove each saying.
- Check more than one source for each fact.

- A ring around the moon means that there will be rain or snow the next day.

- If a groundhog sees its shadow on February 2, winter will last six more weeks.

- Pinecones close up when rain is on the way.

- When the barometer falls low, prepare for a blow.

3. Ms. Incredible

Goal: Write and illustrate a newspaper story about a female athlete with incredible ability.

- Choose a sport you know well.

- Think about an amazing skill that would help any athlete in that sport.

- Imagine the headlines about this athlete; then write her story. Include an illustration of the athlete's skill.

TIPS

- Make your athlete interesting and funny.
- Add details about the sport.

Copyright © Houghton Mifflin Company. All rights reserved.

Name _____

1. Problem-Solving Skit

Goal: Write and perform a skit in which characters identify and solve a problem.

TIPS

- Choose a problem that has a clear solution.
- When writing the skit, follow a story structure.

Decide on the Problem

With a small group of classmates brainstorm a list of problems the characters in your skit could solve. Think about

- problems you have solved
- problems in which you overcame obstacles to reach a goal
- problems that would be interesting to your audience

Choose one problem from your list for your skit. Think about a way to act out this problem and its solution.

Write Your Skit

Write a short script for your skit. Think about

- how many characters you need so that every member of the group participates
- what each character will say
- what part each character will have in solving the problem

Assign a character to each member of your group. Practice your skit together. Make any necessary changes to improve it.

Share What You Know

Once you feel comfortable with your skit, perform it for the class. Speak clearly so that everyone can hear you. Ask the class if they can tell you what the problem was and how the characters solved it.

Copyright © Houghton Mifflin Company. All rights reserved.

Name_____

2. Go, Team, Go!

Goal: Predict what a favorite team or athlete will do next season.

A common saying in sports is "Wait until next year." People say this because they hope that the next season will be better. Choose your favorite sports team or athlete. Use a prediction chart, like the one on page 4 of the Practice Book, to list details about your subject, such as

- talents and abilities

- past achievements

- changes that might affect performance

Then write a prediction of how that team or athlete will do next season.

TIPS

- Choose a sports team or athlete you know a lot about.

- State your prediction clearly.

3. Alternative Solutions

Goal: Choose a different solution for the problem in the selection and rewrite the ending to show your solution.

TIPS

- Choose a solution that could actually have worked in the story.

- Supply specific details of how your solution would work.

In *My Name Is María Isabel,* María Isabel solves a problem by writing how she feels in an essay. List three other ways María Isabel could have solved her problem or achieved her goal. Choose one and rewrite the ending of the story so that her problem gets solved using your solution. Be sure your ending fits the story.

Copyright © Houghton Mifflin Company. All rights reserved.

Name _____

1. A Change in Cast

Goal: Change the plot of a story by adding, removing, or changing a main character. Present your new story.

Choose the Story

If a new character is added or a main character is changed, plots can take unexpected turns.

- Choose a favorite story and list the main characters.

- Map out the plot on a story map.

Make one of the following changes:

- Take out a main character.

- Replace a main character with a new character.

- Add a new character.

- Change something important about a main character.

TIPS

- Be sure changes to the plot fit the characters.

- Think about whether a new conflict would result from your character change.

Plot the Effects

Using a new story map, show how your change will affect the plot. Think about how your change affects other characters, the conflict, and the resolution of the conflict.

Share What You Know

Decide how to present your work to the class. You might:

- Use the story maps or act out a key scene to show "before" and "after."

- Retell the story or draw a comic strip with its new ending.

Copyright © Houghton Mifflin Company. All rights reserved.

Name _____

**Theme
Paperback**

2. *Who Stole* The Wizard of Oz?

Goal: Have a classmate find errors in your summary of the story.

- Write a detailed summary of *Who Stole* The Wizard of Oz?

- Rewrite the summary, changing some of the important elements in the story, such as events, facts, or dialogue.

- Have a classmate identify and rewrite the false elements to make them true.

- Compare and discuss the summaries.

TIPS
- Don't make your changes too obvious.
- Stick to main events rather than unimportant ones.

3. Prize-Winning Problem Solvers

Goal: Use a Problem/Solution chart to analyze how a Nobel Peace Prize recipient worked toward the solution of a problem.

Mother Teresa (1979)

Bishop Desmond Tutu (1984)

Kim Dae Jung (2000)

Choose someone from above.

- Find out why he or she was awarded the Nobel Peace Prize.

- Analyze what he or she did, using a Problem/Solution chart.

- Tell what steps he or she took to resolve the problem.

TIPS
- Choose a major problem.
- Put the steps in the sequence that he or she took to solve the problem.

Copyright © Houghton Mifflin Company. All rights reserved.

Name _____

1. From Parts to Whole

Goal: Divide the tasks of a project among several group members or small teams and work together to complete the project.

Choose the Project

Dividing responsibility for a project gets it done. First, as a group, choose a project that has several parts or steps. You might:

- Create a reading mural made up of several different panels.

- Create an alphabet or number book for younger students.

- Construct an illustrated time line for a scientific discovery or invention, such as the telephone.

Division of Labor

Divide the tasks among your small teams. Use these guidelines:

- Each task should be about equal in work and easy to understand.

- The teams will need someone to track and organize all the parts.

- Focus on working together.

Share What You Know

Put the parts together. Then give an oral presentation to the class. Have a spokesperson from each team explain how his or her group worked together to complete the project.

TIPS

- When choosing or assigning tasks, consider the talents of team members.

- Be sure that all the tasks in the project are assigned or chosen.

Copyright © Houghton Mifflin Company. All rights reserved.

Name_____

2. Beyond the Frame

Goal: Study a work of art and report your conclusions.

With a classmate, find a color reproduction of an interesting work of art. Separately, draw conclusions from what you see. Use a chart like the one on Practice Book page 39 to help you. Share your conclusions with your classmate and talk about how your conclusions are similar and different, and why.

TIPS

- Make notes about your first impressions.
- Support your conclusions with details from the art.

3. The Spelling Dragon

Goal: Create a board game.

Draw a dragon shape on a large piece of poster board. Put plenty of twists in its body. Divide the dragon into sections large enough for a colored marker. Label the dragon's head as *Start* and the tail as *Finish*.

TIPS

- Make sure you have 19 or fewer spaces.
- Each player uses a different color marker.

Write each of your 20 spelling words on page 44 of the Practice Book on a separate card. The first player draws a card from the spelling card pile. The first player then asks the classmate to the right to spell that word. If the classmate spells it correctly, he or she moves one space. If not, the classmate stays on the same space. Play continues until someone has reached the finish line, or the dragon's tail.

Copyright © Houghton Mifflin Company. All rights reserved.

Name_____

1. Open Your Ears!

Goal: Listen to a new kind of music and respond to it in a creative way.

Choose the Music

Do you have a favorite kind of music? In this activity, you'll find out about a different kind of music. Choose one of the following kinds to research.

- classical
- folk
- country
- jazz

Respond to the Music

Once you have chosen a kind of music, become familiar with one song or musical piece. Let the music inspire you to create something. You might:

TIPS

- Choose a style of music that is new to you.
- Relate your creative piece closely to the music.

- Make a drawing, using colors suggested by the music.
- Write a poem to be read to the music.
- Create movements for a dance.

Share the Response

Share your creative work with your classmates. As you share:

- Play the music that inspired you.
- Explain what you heard in the music that led to your work.
- Tell how the experience broadened your musical interests.

Copyright © Houghton Mifflin Company. All rights reserved.

Name_____

2. Sequels and Structures

Goal: Write a sequel to *Sing to the Stars.*

In *Sing to the Stars,* Ephram gains new confidence. At the same time, Mr. Washington seems to regain his. What if the story continued, but contained a new problem? Write a short sequel using a story map to outline the plot. When you finish writing, share your sequel in a small group.

TIPS

- Your story should have a beginning, middle, and end.

- Make sure that the problem can be solved by the character(s).

3. Making Music

Goal: Create and play musical instruments.

A plastic container with an old balloon stretched over it held on with rubber bands makes a drum. Plastic bottles with varying amounts of water that you blow across to make different pitches sound like a flute. Get together with your group to try out these instruments. Each drum or water bottle will have a different sound. Demonstrate your instruments for the class. Then show them how you play together.

TIPS

- Use clean, recyclable materials.

- Come up with a pattern for your group to play during a presentation.

Copyright © Houghton Mifflin Company. All rights reserved.

Name_____

1. A Better Way

Goal: Write and perform a play that shows a peaceful resolution.

Map the Problem

How can you settle disagreements without fighting? Working in a small group, write and perform a play about a peaceful solution to a disagreement. Follow these steps:

- Think of a situation, based on your experiences, that often leads to a disagreement.

- Put the situation into play form. Write out dialogue and actions for each character.

- Assign roles.

TIPS

- Base the disagreement on realistic situations.

- Make the characters and dialogue believable.

- Try to choose a solution that helps both sides.

Choose the Solution

Add a peaceful solution to your play. Use one of these solutions, or another that comes to mind:

- compromising, each side gives up something

- both sides apologizing

- deciding by the flip of a counter

- asking someone outside of the disagreement to decide

Present Your Play

Present your play to the class. At the end of your play, talk with your audience about the disagreement and the peaceful solution. Ask your audience to suggest other peaceful solutions.

Copyright © Houghton Mifflin Company. All rights reserved.

Name _____

2. Civil Rights Quilt

Goal: Assemble a paper quilt of civil rights activists.

Research the lives of each activist listed below. Then draw their pictures, add brief biographical paragraphs, and mount the portraits in a quilt pattern on a colorful backing.

TIPS

- Indicate what country each person comes from.

- State who each person is, what he or she accomplished, and when.

Rosa Parks	Steve Biko	César Chávez
Ida B. Wells	Frederick Douglass	Peter Zenger
Susan B. Anthony	Mahatma Gandhi	Harriet Tubman

3. The Inspiration, Poetry

Goal: Find and recite poetry that might have inspired people to become civil rights activists.

TIPS

- Recite the poem in a stirring manner.

- Think about how the poem's ideas affect you personally.

Poetry can reach out to others. For example, Langston Hughes (1902–1967) shared in his poems what he felt about being an African American without full civil rights.

- Find a Langston Hughes poem, or one by another poet, in which the poet expresses similar feelings.

- Recite the poem with your group. Then explain how it might have caused readers to become civil rights activists.

Copyright © Houghton Mifflin Company. All rights reserved.

Name_____

1. The Benefits of Biography

> **Goal:** Hold a panel discussion on the purposes and benefits of reading biographies.

Go to the Source

Why do people read biographies? For ideas:

- Recall a biography you especially liked.

- Reread or skim it. List the qualities that most appeal to you.

- Highlight the qualities you would look for in other biographies.

Make Your Argument

Prepare your ideas for the panel discussion. Organize your thoughts about biographies into categories. For example, people read biographies

- to learn (about a period of time, career, or field of study)

- to be inspired

- to find a role model

- to satisfy curiosity

Discuss Your Thoughts

Hold a panel discussion. Share your ideas on the benefits of reading biographies. Follow these guidelines:

TIPS

- Think through your ideas.

- Use examples to back up your opinions.

- Choose a moderator to guide the discussion.

- Have the moderator pose questions, such as, "Should students be required to read biographies, and if so, why?"

- Invite questions from the audience after the discussion.

Copyright © Houghton Mifflin Company. All rights reserved.

Name_____

Theme
Paperback

2. *The Wreck of the* Ethie

Goal: Judge whether the fictional version of the shipwreck of the *Ethie* is true to the spirit of the real shipwreck.

The Wreck of the Ethie is fiction based on fact. Use a judgment chart like the one on Practice Book page 124 to help you decide whether the author remained true to the spirit of the actual event. Think about which story elements changed and which remained the same. Decide whether the differences make the story clearer or more exciting. When you finish your chart, write a short conclusion that summarizes your opinion.

TIPS

• Give specific reasons to support your judgment.

• Consider all sides before forming an opinion.

3. Appealing for Help

TIPS

Goal: Write a letter to a recording artist asking him or her to appear at a benefit for a charitable cause.

• Choose an artist that might already have an interest in your cause.

• Use persuasive words.

Think of a charitable cause that is important to you, and do some research to learn more about it. Write to a recording artist asking him or her to perform at a benefit for this cause. Follow these guidelines:

• Clearly state what you want.

• Include at least three strong reasons for the artist to perform.

• Use positive and polite language.

• Summarize your reasons and ask for a response.

Copyright © Houghton Mifflin Company. All rights reserved.

Name_____

1. Equipped for Baseball

Goal: Work in small groups to explain and illustrate a reference source on baseball equipment.

Choose the Items

To help a newcomer, make an easy-to-use reference source that explains different pieces of baseball equipment.

- Brainstorm a list of baseball equipment.
- Write the name of each item on an index card.
- Divide the cards among the group.

Research Their Uses

Consult encyclopedias and sports books.

- Make notes on the index cards.
- Name the source that gave you the information.
- On separate sheets of paper, sketch the items and write a one-paragraph explanation for each.

TIPS

- Divide the writing and drawing tasks among your group.
- Choose a publishing method that presents the information clearly and easily.

Publish Your Work

Decide how to present your information. You could create

- a sports dictionary
- a baseball magazine
- sports flash cards

Share your work with the class.

Copyright © Houghton Mifflin Company. All rights reserved.

Name_____

2. Heroes

Goal: Write an essay about someone that you consider a hero.

Reread the selections and list all the qualities that make up a hero. Then, think of someone in your life or in history that you feel shows the qualities of a hero. Write an essay explaining why he or she is a hero.

TIPS

• Take notes describing how the person shows each characteristic.

• Use details from the person's life to support your ideas.

3. The Fact or Opinion Game

Goal: Create a fact and opinion board game.

With a partner, make a set of cards with a statement about baseball on each one. Some should be facts and some should be opinions. Check each fact.

• Make the board on poster board. Be sure it has a start, a finish, and multiple squares to travel on.

• Rules should describe how each player draws a card from the deck, identifies the statement as fact or opinion, and if correct, moves along the board.

TIPS

• Use signal words for opinions.

• Provide an answer key so players can check their guesses.

• In the deck, include chances for players to hit a double (advance two places), a triple (three places), and a home run (four places), or to steal a base (advance one place).

• Play the game with your partner.

Copyright © Houghton Mifflin Company. All rights reserved.

Name_____

1. Kodiak Island Experts

Goal: Take part in a question and answer session about Kodiak Island.

TIPS

- Use your notes to guide you. Do not read from your notes.

- You should have most of the information committed to memory.

- Be sure to answer your questions completely.

Choose Your Questions

You and a group of classmates are going to become experts on Kodiak Island. As a group, brainstorm a list of questions about Kodiak Island. Reread *Salmon Summer* and read other reference sources to help you. Choose one member of your group as moderator. He or she will ask the questions. Each group member should choose two questions to research.

Become an Expert

- When you have chosen your two questions, research Kodiak Island and take notes on each question.

- Once you have completed your research, make notes on index cards that you will use to answer your questions.

- The moderator should write out each question on a slip of paper and put all the questions into a jar or box.

Inform the Class

Have a question and answer session for your class.

- The moderator will ask volunteers to draw a question from the jar or box.

- The moderator reads the question aloud, and the expert whose question is read stands and answers the question.

Copyright © Houghton Mifflin Company. All rights reserved.

Name_____

2. Hidden Ocean Treasure

Goal: Gain ability in giving and receiving directions.

Write clear directions for a classmate to find a hidden object.

- Find an object in the classroom that has to do with the ocean.

- Hide your object somewhere in the classroom.

- Write directions to find the object using words like *start, right, left, up, down, first, next,* and *last.*

- Once your partner has found the object, switch roles.

TIPS

- Choose an object that is small enough to hide easily, but not too small to be found.

- If your classmate does not find the object, revise your directions until he or she finds it.

3. Catch and Release: A Debate

Goal: Debate catch-and-release fishing.

TIPS

- Understand your opponent's arguments so that you can respond to them.

- Be persuasive in your arguments.

Pollution and other factors have decreased the population of some fish. One suggestion to stop this decline is catch-and-release fishing. With a partner, research this topic and interview people who fish. Make a chart listing the reasons for and against catch-and-release fishing. Learn the arguments for, and ask your partner to learn the arguments against the idea. Then hold a debate. Invite your classmates to vote on the issue after hearing both sides.

Copyright © Houghton Mifflin Company. All rights reserved.

Name _____

1. The Answer Machine

Goal: Create an answer machine.

Build the Machine

Working in a small group, make an answer machine.

TIPS

- Divide the work equally among your group.

- Make notes of reference sources for the answers.

- Design and make a machine from a carton or box. Decorate it with dials and buttons.

- Provide a slot into which classmates can drop their question cards.

- Create question cards for your classmates to fill out. Each card should have space for the classmate's name, the topic, the question, and the answer.

Ask for Questions

Meet with your group to choose a nature topic.

- Put up an announcement listing the nature topic you will focus on. Add a pouch to hold a supply of question cards.

- Invite classmates to use the question cards. Tell them to place the cards into the slot on your machine.

- Divide the cards among your group and research the answers.

Deliver the Answers

Decide how to present your answers. Some possibilities:

- Display the answers on a poster in your classroom.

- Hold a question and answer session with the class.

Copyright © Houghton Mifflin Company. All rights reserved.

Name_____

2. The Good Side of Volcanoes

Goal: Research the aftereffects of volcanic eruptions to determine benefits.

What are some benefits of volcanic eruptions?

- Research volcanoes to find the benefits.

- Fill out a main idea and details chart like the one on page 208 of the Practice Book.

- Write an essay using your chart. Share your essay with a classmate.

TIPS

- The main idea of each paragraph should be related to the topic of the entire selection.

- Each supporting detail should connect to the main idea.

Theme Paperback

3. *Water Hole: Life in a Rescued Tropical Forest*

Goal: Record your impressions of one hour spent "observing" the water hole.

- Choose one time of the day you could be observing the water hole and reread that section in *Water Hole: Life in a Rescued Tropical Forest.*

- Make mental notes of your impressions as you read.

- Express those impressions in art, poetry, or another kind of creative work. Share your work with the class.

TIPS

- Try to capture the tempo or rhythm of the movements you observe.

- Express your personal reactions to what you see and hear.

Copyright © Houghton Mifflin Company. All rights reserved.

Name_____

1. From Small Things

Goal: Learn how a small step like recycling paper can help improve water supplies.

> **TIPS**
> - Focus on causes and effects.
> - Show how small steps can make a difference.

Find the Facts

Can little things make a difference? To answer that question, work with a group to research and make connections. The "little thing" is recycling paper. The difference it might make is protecting water supplies. Begin by researching and taking notes on the following:

- deforestation
- soil erosion
- fertilizers and pesticides

Make the Connections

Discuss the following questions with your group. Write your conclusions. What is the connection between

- recycling paper and deforestation?
- deforestation and soil erosion?
- fertilizers and pesticides, and water pollution?

Share What You Learned

Decide how your group will present your conclusions:

- a written report, with each group member writing a different step
- a chart showing cause and effect
- a picture essay

Copyright © Houghton Mifflin Company. All rights reserved.

Name_____

2. Caleb's Story

Goal: Retell the story from Caleb's point of view.

> **TIPS**
> - Include details that would be important to Caleb.
> - Describe feelings he might have had.

Different people have different versions of the same story. In *Skylark*, the reader gets the story from Anna's point of view.

- Write the story the way Caleb might have told it.
- Use what you know and the details of the selection to make inferences about how events affected Caleb. Use an inference chart like the one on page 223 of the Practice Book.

3. Nature: Friend or Foe?

Goal: Write a speech about nature.

> **TIPS**
> - List ways nature is helpful or harmful before you write.
> - Use persuasive and interesting language.

In this theme, you read about how nature can be both a friend and a foe. Write a speech about either way. In your speech, be sure to

- state the main idea first
- list the important facts or events in a clear order
- include interesting and important details that develop the topic
- end with a closing sentence
- display the answer on the poster in your classroom
- hold a class question and answer session

Copyright © Houghton Mifflin Company. All rights reserved.

Problem/Solution Chart

Page _____

Problem: _____

Steps: _____

_____

Solution: _____

Page _____

Problem: _____

Steps: _____

_____

Solution: _____

Page _____

Problem: _____

Steps: _____

_____

Solution: _____

Page _____

Problem: _____

Steps: _____

_____

Solution: _____

Copyright © Houghton Mifflin Company. All rights reserved.

Conclusions Chart

page _____

_____

_____

Details
_____
_____
_____
_____

Conclusions
_____
_____
_____
_____

page _____

_____

_____

Details
_____
_____
_____
_____

Conclusions
_____
_____
_____
_____

page _____

_____

_____

Details
_____
_____
_____
_____

Conclusions
_____
_____
_____
_____

Copyright © Houghton Mifflin Company. All rights reserved.

Story Map

Title: _____

Characters	Setting

Plot

Problem

What Happens

Ending

Copyright © Houghton Mifflin Company. All rights reserved.

Main Idea and Details Chart

Topic: _____

Page _____ Main Idea	Page _____ Main Idea
_____	_____
_____	_____
Supporting Details	**Supporting Details**
_____	_____
_____	_____
_____	_____
_____	_____
_____	_____
_____	_____
_____	_____
Page _____ Main Idea	**Page _____ Main Idea**
_____	_____
_____	_____
Supporting Details	**Supporting Details**
_____	_____
_____	_____
_____	_____
_____	_____
_____	_____
_____	_____

Copyright © Houghton Mifflin Company. All rights reserved.

Judgments Chart

Question: _____ **?**

Copyright © Houghton Mifflin Company. All rights reserved.